Feel Good About Yourself

Empowering 'Feel Good Book' Packed With
Self Improvement Techniques To
Immediately Build Your Confidence
And Self Esteem

Boost Your Happiness Levels Today!

A FeelFabToday Guide
By Rachel Robins

Feel Good About Yourself

All Rights Reserved

Cover and internal vector images
credited to: © Li Wu / Dreamstime

ISBN-13: 978-1494481223

ISBN-10: 1494481227

Table of Contents

1

How This Book Will Help You Feel Good About Yourself

Ever wonder what confident, happy, outgoing people have in common?

Well, we're about the show you. We'll guide you through some of the best, easy to use, step by step methods for how to feel great, boost your mood and achieve daily positivity.

When it comes to feeling good about yourself, there's no flash new gimmicks; just tried and tested methods that actually work. When they're used in the correct way, they can be extremely powerful.

What you'll discover in this book:

- ♥ **What** you *really* need to do to feel good
- ♥ **Why** these methods are incredibly powerful and work so well
- ♥ **How** to get started and take steps that really make a difference
- ♥ **Stop** procrastinating, worrying, or being mean to yourself

- ♥ **Start** taking action and see surprising, awesome results
- ♥ **Easy** ways to take control of your life and change your outlook
- ♥ **Fresh** ideas to build your confidence
- ♥ **Empowering** new habits you can start building today
- ♥ **Fast** acting techniques to de-clutter and remove negativity
- ♥ **Simple** steps to turn your dreams into reality
- ♥ **Instant** ways to achieve good mood moments whenever you want
- ♥ **Step by step** actionable ideas

The objective of this book is to help you stop treading water and take action. When you begin to do the right things, and practice them daily, you'll begin to see amazing results.

If you're just beginning your journey, then you'll be introduced to some exciting, new ideas on how to feel good about yourself. If you've explored some of these subjects before, then you'll discover inspiring reminders and tips about the best feel good techniques, plus fresh ideas, and how to use them to great effect.

Our aim is to help you to evaluate how you currently see yourself, and to understand why a negative self image is both misinformed and harmful. We look at how to overcome damaging self-beliefs using positive, practical steps so you can feel good about yourself permanently. It is our intention that when you follow the techniques, methods and tips in this book, you will be able to:

- ♥ **Stop** self-doubt and overcome negativity
- ♥ **Start** to feel energized and focused
- ♥ **Feel** good about yourself everyday
- ♥ **Develop** simple skills to achieve daily and long-lasting positivity

We hope you'll receive heaps of value from this book, so let's dive in and get started…

2

Are You Getting In Your Own Way?

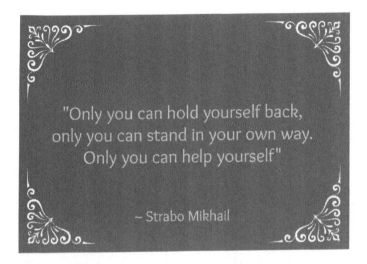

"Only you can hold yourself back,
only you can stand in your own way.
Only you can help yourself"

~ Strabo Mikhail

In this chapter we'll explore the ways in which you may be getting in your own way, holding yourself back, and unconsciously preventing yourself from feeling good. We'll examine the reality of "garbage in, garbage out", and how to avoid stock-piling your own mental garbage.

Plus, we'll explore ways in which other people's negativity can affect your feelings, and more importantly, how to avoid letting negativity into your life.

Holding Yourself Back

As a starting point, it's important to identify the primary causes of why you don't feel good about yourself.

It can be too easy to rely on excuses for not doing, being and having exactly what we want in our lives. It can be too easy to blame others, or blame the circumstances we find ourselves in. And yet, if we are really honest with ourselves, it can often be self-defeating, negative self-talk that is responsible for holding us back.

However, this book is not simply about telling you to 'snap out of it'. Whilst we all have moments of being self absorbed, and need a nudge in the right direction to move forward with a positive mindset, there are situations when our personal issues are much more serious. If you have overwhelming issues with low self-esteem, anxiety, or depression, then simply 'snapping out of it' is not an option. You need to identity and implement more robust and appropriate techniques to tackle the seriousness of these problems.

Throughout this book we'll investigate and consider how to use various methods for tackling low self-esteem and improving your confidence levels. Be mindful, though, that you could have underlying health issues that affect how you feel, where processional medical treatment would be beneficial, to assist you with improving how you feel both physically and emotionally.

Techniques in this book may then be helpful when combined with other treatments or processes.

However, there are many highly effective, stand-alone techniques that can benefit the majority of people, helping them to feel good about themselves on a day to day basis.

Your brain is an amazingly powerful tool.
If you use it well, it will serve you well.

Your mind, if left unchecked, can be destructive. Like an unruly child, it will benefit from good controls and positive education.

When you focus on negative issues and allow self-sabotaging thoughts to control your world, then you will struggle to ever feel truly good about yourself. Learning to re-focus your thoughts in a supportive and self-caring manner is not always easy, but extremely powerful once learnt and maintained.

Firstly, we'll look at the impact that self-limiting beliefs and negative self-talk can have on your ability to feel good about yourself, and how to overcome these obstacles.

Self-Limiting Or Unrealistic Beliefs

A self-limiting or unrealistic belief is a label that only we can genuinely apply to ourselves.

Such feelings may come from comparing yourself to an unattainable goal or image that is just not realistic (often someone else's idea of what you should be). These types of comparison will never be helpful, and will keep holding you back. The disappointment of not achieving an unrealistic goal means you keep getting in your own way and then reinforce negative feelings toward yourself.

If you've been subjected to long periods of criticism or negativity, it can be hard to break a pattern of self-doubt or low self-esteem. Start by silencing the inner critic – this is the most damaging of voices, and will have the most life-changing impact when that voice is silenced.

You may find yourself trying too hard to be the person you think others want you to be. Or, maybe you compare yourself to some other person or persons you consider to be perfect or ideal?

So what are *your* self-limiting beliefs? Do you hear yourself saying any of the following or making similar statements?

- ♥ I'm not smart enough to do...
- ♥ I don't have any special talents or skills
- ♥ Why don't I look more like X

- ♥ Everyone else is smarter / more capable than me
- ♥ Why can't I be more like my sister / friend / famous person
- ♥ If only I could do better, then maybe X would like me
- ♥ I'll never be able to do…

Unfortunately, when you repeatedly allow negative self-chatter to go on inside your head it can become a self fulfilling prophecy. Your mind will find evidence to support these limiting beliefs and keep 'proving' you right.

To successfully tackle the issue of self-limiting beliefs, you may need to address and/or remove the source of the issue. That may potentially mean removing or reducing contact with any perpetrators of the criticism/negativity that holds you back.

This could be a person who is still in your life, or their voice that fills your head with 'their' thoughts. By understanding their impact on your self-worth, and tackling these negative effects, you will be in a better position to take control, learn to speak up, take a stand, and show that you are good enough.

Obviously, there are times when we all need to be realistic about our abilities. For example, if you're tone deaf, then you are not going to become a world-class opera singer. If you lack patience and are not comfortable around groups of people, you are unlikely to make a great teacher.

However, most beliefs that hold us back, and prevent us from achieving our personal potential or feeling good about ourselves, are negative, self-limiting beliefs. Despite these destructive habits, the good news is that these habits can be successfully turned around, allowing you to build a positive, caring relationship with yourself.

"Your life is a garden,
your thoughts are the seeds.
If your life isn't awesome,
you've been watering the weeds."
~ Terry Prince

Start by making a list of all your self-limiting beliefs.

Then, take each one individually and explore the reasons for those beliefs – when did they start, how often do they occur, what or who triggers them, how do you feel when you think these thoughts?

Take the time to challenge each negative statement and turn it into something manageable and positive.

For example:

Negative statement - I'm rubbish with finances and figure work.

<u>Replace with</u> - I've struggled with figures and managing my finances so far, but I'm going to enroll in an evening course to learn the basics and take control.

Negative statement - I'll never be in a healthy, loving relationship.

<u>Replace with</u> - I haven't found 'the one' yet, but I'm going to start by respecting myself more. Then, I'll arrange to join some new groups and hopefully meet new people with similar interests.

Negative statement - Why can't I be more like (insert the person's name you are comparing yourself to)?

<u>Replace with</u> - I like the fact that (name) is popular and outgoing. I'm happy with who I am, however, I'm going to practice some self-confidence building techniques so I can learn to be more outgoing.

Reminding yourself to turn a negative statement into a positive and proactive one can take time. However, even small steps can make a big difference.

You could 'fine' yourself each time you catch yourself making a negative statement. For example, you pay a small fee into a 'positivity pot'. You could reward yourself with a mini 'gift' each time you catch yourself going straight into a positive, solution oriented statement. That way, you're focused on maintaining the momentum and keeping positive thoughts at front of your mind (so no excuse for slipping back into bad habits!).

Practice this mind-set often enough and it will begin to become an empowering and affirming habit, which will continually lead you toward feeling good about yourself.

"There is nothing to do except to be just who you are.
You have the right to feel beautiful and enjoy it."
~ Miguel Ruiz

Negative Self-Talk

Negative self-talk is destructive. Reversing these damaging words will enable you to feel better about yourself and respond to people/situations in an intelligent, controlled and positive manner.

There may be times when you're feeling stressed, anxious, dissatisfied, or depressed and, therefore, negative thoughts will be more likely to affect you. Understanding how to dispel such thoughts, and practicing techniques to overcome them, can take patience and time, but are so worth the effort.

**Take some time out to identify the
negative statements you make to yourself.**

**These statements will invariably be
distorted, magnified, incorrect and unsupportive.**

Dealing with the source of any self-esteem issues is critical to challenging the way you value yourself and speak to yourself. Later in the book we will tackle the way in which others can deeply affect our self belief, confidence, and ability to feel good about ourselves.

When you acknowledge that any negative thought patterns can be indicative of self-destructive behavior, and recognize and commit to the need for change, then you're in a strong position to make a permanent shift. You'll then be able to concentrate on using motivating techniques and finding ways to view things from a supportive, self-caring perspective.

*"Healing may not be so much about getting better, as
about letting go of everything that isn't you - all of the
expectations, all of the beliefs - and becoming who you are."
~ Rachel Naomi Remen*

**Listen to how you talk to yourself - what are you
habitually saying? Can you hear yourself saying
things such as:**

- I can't do...
- I'm not worthy of...
- I wish I was not so...
- I'm a failure
- I'm so stupid
- I'm not good enough

Breaking the pattern of destructive, negative self-talk can be difficult at first; however, the result is well worth the effort. **Commit to an intention to break the negative head-chatter.** There are many techniques you can use to create new, empowering ways of communicating with yourself, such as:

- Positive quotes and reminders highlighted around your home or office.
- Refer regularly to self-help books that motivate and inspire you.
- Compile a note book with detailed proactive steps you will take.
- Diarize and record your thoughts, actions and achievements.
- Daily gratitude statements, self praise and recognition for small successes.
- Discover ways to laugh or smile at the world and yourself.

♥ Positive affirmations so your subconscious can focus on self-nurturing beliefs.

♥ Visualization to help you move toward your positive new self image.

It's important to realize that switching off your critical voice (and replacing it with a new supportive voice) takes effort, time, and commitment. It's not something you can just do a few times and expect to experience a massive change.

You could start with scheduling a 'Positively Positive Day'. Schedule one day a week where *NO* negative talk is permitted. Try out some of the following:

♥ Plan for it the night before.

♥ When you wake, clearly state your intentions to only allow positive thoughts and gestures all day.

♥ Wear a favorite outfit, something you feel good in.

♥ Paint your nails a beautiful color or wear a bright scarf – something to keep reminding you that you're in a 'Positively Positive Day'.

♥ Build in some mini 'me-time' activities and things that make you smile.

♥ Use positive words to replace gloomy ones.

♥ Smile at everyone you meet.

♥ Pay others a compliment.

- ♥ Do something unexpected and nice for someone you care about, or possibly a stranger.
- ♥ Banish all negative, self-sabotaging words – stop them in their tracks – they are *NOT* allowed space in your head on this day.
- ♥ Give yourself a mini gift at the end of the day to celebrate.

Even if it doesn't work perfectly, you'll have taken some positive steps. Some ideas may work better than others - just build in more of what works for you. Even if it rains on your new hairdo, you're late for work, the hot water's gone again – don't let such issues sidetrack or stop your 'positive' day. It's all part of the journey, and you can still do all the positive steps, once you've dealt with the daily annoyances.

Building up new ways to approach your day, and discovering ways to ditch the negative head chatter means you're strengthening your positivity 'muscle'.

It's an area you'll need to consistently work on, until you achieve a new, affirming mindset. Developing new, empowering self-talk habits means you can activate a good mood whenever you want *and* then stay positive.

> *"Holding onto anger is like grasping a hot coal*
> *with the intent of throwing it at someone else;*
> *you are the one who gets burned!"*
> *~ Budda*

Garbage In, Garbage Out

The saying **"garbage in, garbage out"** started with computer programming. If you supply a computer with a program that contains nothing more than nonsensical garbage, the computer will only provide the same nonsense in reply to your inquiries.

We can apply this approach to our own lives as well. If someone fills you with negative garbage about how you're not good enough, and you go on to believe this garbage, what you give out may also be negative garbage (including your own self-critical voice). People who make these comments can be extremely damaging to your self esteem, and their opinions should not be allowed to form part of your own self-image. **Try mentally picturing their criticism as garbage and see yourself placing it in a trash bag, securely tying the top shut and tossing it into a dumpster.**

In addition, our knowledge base and thoughts are only as good as the information we choose to feed into our brains. Therefore, if we only watch poor quality television, focus on the tragedies and awfulness in the news, and have meaningless conversations people, then these are the topics brains will focus on.

Alternatively, when we surround ourselves with interesting people, challenge ourselves to learn new things, visit new places, and try out new activities, then we enrich the data we feed into our minds. Instead of 'garbage in, garbage out', we have 'fab stuff in, fab stuff out'!

According to the author and motivational speaker, Jim Rohn, "You are the average of the 5 people you spend the most time with". Therefore, the people you choose to spend your time with can have a direct impact on how you feel.

Here's some worthwhile, feel-good stuff to try:

- Instead of watching the news programs, select a book about someone inspiring or a subject you'd like to learn more about.
- Compile some motivating music tracks for when you exercise or do the chores.
- Arrange a get-together with friends and share plans for the future.
- Commit to attending a new class for something you've wanted to do for ages.
- Pick 3 self development books (audio if you're too busy to read) and make notes on areas you can act on straight away.
- Spend time with people who energize and inspire you.
- Check out Internet forums/communities that focus on interesting topics.
- Volunteer or get involved in your local community projects.

♥ Join a local business group for networking opportunities.

**Ask yourself the question –
does this activity really benefit me?**

It's obvious that we can't always be engaged in meaningful activities, and it's definitely good to veg out or do something silly from time to time. However, it can be helpful to check that you are spending at least some quality time on activities that enhance you as a person, rather than drag you down or keep you in a stagnant place.

> *"The whole purpose of education is to
> turn mirrors into windows."*
> *~Sydney J. Harris*

Avoiding Negativity

We've all encountered negative people. Being stuck with them for any length of time can be extremely draining and offer little or no benefit.

If you spend too much time with people who are constantly seeing the negative in everything, then you can start to feel that way too! However, when you spend time with positive, cheerful people, you can't help but pick up on their positive energy and feel good. By spending time with people who support you and want to see you do well, you can't help but feel good about yourself!

In terms of self-awareness, it's important to understand what specifically triggers your negative emotions:

- Are there specific situations you find stressful?
- Do you always try and avoid conflict/ confrontation?
- Are there certain negative people you would prefer to avoid?

Some people will seek to control others, but this often has damaging results. If this happens to you, do you feel as though your thoughts and actions are your own, or someone else's? Are you being true to your personal values and making choices for yourself, or are you reacting in ways that you think are expected of you?

- Stop and consider who exactly you are trying to please.
- What power does that person/s hold over you?
- What is the worst that could happen to you if you did not please that person?
- How do you feel when you please that person?

◆ How do you feel when you do something for yourself instead?

Negative people may try to get you down, by being critical or unpleasant. However, you have a choice as to how you react to them. Accept that you do not deserve to be their emotional punch bag.

"Fairy tales are more than true:
not because they tell us that dragons exist,
but because they tell us that
dragons can be beaten."
~ Neil Gaiman

Unfortunately, we can't always avoid the naysayers or those who have a negative outlook, and to a certain extent, we need to try and be tolerant. Even people who are generally negative, or who we find difficult, have their good points. You may need to develop some coping strategies for spending any length of time with them, providing their negativity does not become personal toward you.

Finally if their negativity becomes too much, or becomes personal, then you have the choice to reduce the time you spend with them, or drop them from your life entirely.

After all, you absolutely do not have to accept someone being nasty toward you.

It's far better to surround yourself with those who can motivate, support, encourage and inspire you.

These people will help you to grow, take positive action in your life and feel good about yourself!

It's also an important point to ensure that we are not the ones who are being critical of others, and adversely affecting *them* with negativity. If you stop and listen to yourself do you find yourself nagging at your kids too much, fault-finding with your partner, criticizing other family members, carping on at colleagues, or being cutting to your friends?

Obviously, there are times when people get on our nerves or warrant criticism. However try to ensure it's well placed and constructive, in both its tone and usefulness. If you find yourself constantly in critical mode, then you could be the one ultimately affecting how others feel about themselves.

Take time to check your words and intentions.

"Actions, good thoughts, and positive energy,
speak louder than judgmental words
and are the most powerful tools you can use
when working toward a better world."
~ Madisyn Taylor

At this point, it's also worth mentioning the negative impact we can have on ourselves, especially if we overdo things. Burn-out can cause us to dwell on the negative, as we don't have the mental energy to do otherwise.

Unfortunately, we may not be able to avoid this completely when we're rushing round with ultra busy lives. However, if you recognize the symptoms early enough, then you can take appropriate action.

Take time out to do something relaxing, or something that makes you smile, even if it's only briefly:

- ♥ Ask someone to give you a foot rub, or book a massage for the weekend.
- ♥ Read a chapter from an inspirational book.
- ♥ Go for a walk somewhere soothing.
- ♥ Remind yourself of a forgotten meditation technique.
- ♥ Read old letters or thank you notes from friends or loved ones.

- ♥ Watch something that makes you laugh.
- ♥ Make pancakes with the kids.

These are just a few ideas to get you thinking about something positive (and squashing out any negativity). You can probably come up with a whole lot more ideas that work for you, simply by asking the question "What enjoyable, funny, relaxing things can I do, can I read, can I listen, to that will make me feel good about myself?

"Find out who you are and do it on purpose."
~ Dolly Parton

3

Learn To Focus On What You *Can* Control

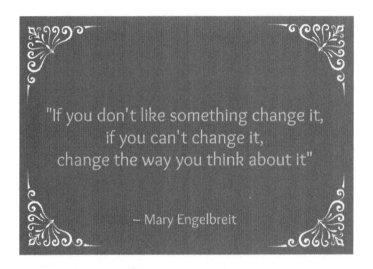

"If you don't like something change it,
if you can't change it,
change the way you think about it"

– Mary Engelbreit

In this chapter we'll identify the events in your life you can control, and those you can't, and we'll explore how to accept and let go of events and situations you can't control. You'll discover how best to take charge, and how to evaluate your choices and priorities.

Plus, we'll checkout the reasons why it's great to say "YES" and when it is great to say "NO", and how to be comfortable with either.

Taking Charge, Prioritizing And Making Great Choices

Controlling Your Choices

There are many things in our lives we can control, and many more that we can't. We cannot control the weather, the passage of time, aging, traffic and bad drivers, death and some illnesses, or rude people. Struggling against something you can't control can make you angry and frustrated, and is inevitably a complete waste of time.

Learning to identify what you can't control, and how you choose to react to these events, will help you to take another step toward feeling good about yourself. Don't waste energy or time reacting to things you can't control. Stay focused on what you're doing, and avoid the temptation to become involved in negative drama going on around you.

> _"You express the truth of your character_
> _with the choice of your actions."_
> _~ Steve Maraboli_

Let's look at one example - how to deal with rude people. These people are often demanding attention, and, for some reason, enjoy making other people feel inferior. It's important to remember that rude people are typically looking for a fight of some kind. Instead of taking the bait and fighting back, be annoying and overwhelm them with kindness or nonchalance. They won't know how to react, and most likely, will leave you alone to look for another rude or reactive person to battle with.

When you choose not to allow yourself to get into a confrontation or get sidetracked, you'll be amazed at how good you feel about yourself. And you never know, some of your kindness may actually rub off on that rude person!

When you identify a situation you can't control, start looking for the so-called silver lining. If you get stuck in a traffic jam, choose to see it as more time to listen to your favorite music, play a self-development CD, or plan out some positive steps you can take toward a goal you've set for yourself. If bad weather keeps you home, choose to see it as keeping you away from a possible accident, and use the time to achieve something you'll feel pleased about instead.

Whilst many situations occur that we can't control, how we choose to react to them is up to us. You can allow the frustration to overwhelm you, or you can choose to reengineer the situation to your benefit. Try to put the situation into perspective, take control, and find an opportunity to achieve something else of profit. You may not have planned to do that activity at that time, but an opportunity presented itself and you took advantage of it!

*"Incredible change happens in your life when you decide to
take control of what you do have power over,
instead of craving control over what you don't."*
~ Steve Maraboli

Every day we are presented with the need to make decisions. Some are small and insignificant; others are large and have potentially major consequences. For the less significant ones, try not to over think. Trust your instincts and move on.

For the more important ones, take time to consider the various consequences, seek advice where necessary, and don't react in the heat of the moment. When you've weighed up the various pros/cons and thought things through in a calm manner, then you should be able to trust your instincts to make the right decision.

**Make sure your choices reflect who you want to be
and help move you forward in the right direction**

At the end of the day, the choices we make in life help to define who we are and where we end up.

*"You have two choices in life...
Choice one is to be the same and be like everyone else...
Choice two is to be yourself and be a difference-maker."*
~ Jazlyn Roehl

Priorities

We all have masses of thing we need to do, and ever growing 'To-Do' lists. Often, we'll have lists for the home and family, ones to manage for work, plus our own personal stuff. However, it's important not to become overwhelmed by them all.

There are 2 key areas to focus on – short and long term priorities. Short-term priorities should focus on achieving the daily/weekly activities that are both regular and one-offs. Long-term priorities focus on areas such as family, relationships, career, travel, lifestyle and creative goals.

It can, therefore, be helpful to create a personal priority system, to identify the key areas you need to focus on. As you cross-off the tasks, you'll be rewarded with a sense of satisfaction, especially when you look back at what you've managed to achieve.

There are many tools available to help you prioritize your lists, enabling you to capture the essential tasks you need to focus on, and, therefore, be more productive. There are both PC based tools and smart-phone apps, which you can update daily – these can even email you with daily reminders. Or you may be more comfortable with a notepad or daily post-it notes. Whichever system you use, if you use it effectively, then it should help you feel good about your short-term achievements, and the successful steps you make toward your long term goals.

To help focus on your priorities, try asking yourself:

Short-term Priorities

- Have I clearly captured all the regular items I need to, so nothing is forgotten?
- Do I have a system to capture the one-off tasks that must be done?
- Do I have a system to capture the non-urgent things that need to be done?
- Can I delegate or remove any of these tasks so I can work on my long-term priorities?
- Can I manage my time better/complete tasks more efficiently?

Long-term Priorities

- Have I clearly identified the longer-term priorities for each area of my life?
- Am I clear how to achieve these, so they don't become swamped by the more urgent short-term lists?
- What can I do differently to achieve these long-term objectives?

Obviously, our priorities and objectives change over time. By capturing them clearly we are able to review them, assess our achievements, and then give ourselves a pat on the back.

We can also check that our 'To-Do' lists are allowing us to stay on track, move forward as we desire, and are focused on what's really important. When you're on top of the things that matter, then you can't help but feel good about yourself!

"The direction you choose to face
determines whether you're standing
at the end or the beginning of a road."
~ Richelle E. Goodrich

When It's Great To Say NO

One key area you can control is how and when you say 'yes' or 'no' to a request. No one wants to disappoint his or her friends, family, or co-workers, but it is not practical to always say "yes" to everything that's asked of you. Often, people feel guilty about saying no, thinking they're letting others down, but then feel even worse when they find themselves overwhelmed and/or in over their head.

Learning to say no can be uncomfortable at first. We often want to be seen as helpful, we worry about seeming rude or causing conflict, and don't want to spoil a relationship for the future. However, it's all about learning to say 'no' in the *right way*. People are usually more understanding than we expect them to be. Be mindful, however, that those who don't show any understanding of your needs may have previously seen you as a doormat, and might not react positively to your new found assertiveness.

By taking charge of the situation, you can establish control. Don't allow anyone push you into agreeing to a request until you've had the opportunity to think about it, and decide if it's okay for you to do.

Establishing your own personal boundaries and limits is really important in terms of feeling good about yourself. You know where your comfort zone lies, and what you're happy/unhappy to take on. Boundaries are similar to property lines, and these boundaries define what we are, or are not, willing to be responsible for.

A quick check-list before saying *NO*:

- Is this request something you want to do?
- Do you have the time to take this on?
- Will the time and energy spent on this request be beneficial to you?
- How will you feel if you agree to this request and then find you can't complete it or do it correctly?
- How will the other person feel if you agree to this request and then can't complete it or do it correctly?
- Are you really comfortable saying "yes" to this request?

- Will something or someone else suffer if you agree to this request?
- Is there someone else more qualified or readily available you can suggest to handle this request instead?

Unfortunately, you can spend far too much time and energy on other people's needs, but at a detriment to yourself. Whilst we all need help from time to time, and sometimes, it's great to help others out, there has to be a balance. Finding the strength to say no is about being respectful to yourself and placing a value on your own time and needs.

"Respect yourself enough to walk away from anything that no longer serves you, grows you, or makes you happy."
~ Robert Tew

Saying no needn't be difficult. It's all about *how* you say no, not the fact that you're actually saying no.

Here are some polite and effective techniques to try:

- I'll have a think about it and get back to you (by taking some time you appear to have given the request due consideration. However don't delay your response unnecessarily).

- ♥ I would normally love to, however, I can't this time as I have a prior commitment (don't hesitate too much, or try to give a long excuse - this gives the other person room to try and change your mind or they may view it as an excuse).
- ♥ Unfortunately, now is not a good time for me. Why don't we reschedule for another time? (This keeps the door open and let's the other person know you're happy to help in the future).
- ♥ I don't think I'm the best person to help with this. Perhaps (name) could help?
- ♥ I can't commit to anything extra at the moment as I'm swamped (you could suggest asking you again in the future, if you're happy to help out another time).
- ♥ I'm afraid I simply can't (useful if someone is being unreasonably insistent).

It might take a bit of time and practice, and you may need to remind yourself not to feel guilty about your new stance. However, once you start to say *NO* to certain requests, then you'll be more in control, have more time to yourself, and should definitely feel good about your new assertive self.

As John C Maxwell, author and speaker on leadership, says, "Learn to say 'no' to the good so you can say 'yes' to the best".

When It's Great To Say YES

In order for us to grow as a person, we need to try new experiences.

Often, we find that we are stuck in rut, stagnating and not going anywhere. Do you feel as though there's something missing in your life, but you're not sure how to change things for the better?

Was there a time recently, when you were asked to do something new but you made an excuse not to get involved? Can you hear yourself saying 'maybe' but then never actually getting round to it? Sound familiar?

- ♥ Maybe I'll join that creative writing class one day.
- ♥ Maybe I'll take up the offer to go out with the walking group.
- ♥ Perhaps next time I'll accept some baby-sitting.
- ♥ Maybe I'll get back to the other mum's about meeting up for coffee.
- ♥ I wonder if they'll ask me to the theatre again.
- ♥ I couldn't do that, I'm too nervous.

Vincent Van Gogh once said, "If you hear a voice within you say 'you cannot paint', then by all means paint, and that voice will be silenced".

Instead of focusing on reason's why you can't do something, or over-thinking your fears, go for it. Say YES!

Be open to all new possibilities, be flexible and take some risks!

By saying YES, you'll make new discoveries. Who knows where these may lead – new friends, new career, new skills, healthier lifestyle, new outlook on life and so on...?

By being open to more possibilities, you'll allow yourself to have so much more fun. Follow your passions, take advantage of new opportunities, and keep saying *YES* to what you know or think you'd love to do. Go have an adventure...

"The sweaty players in the game of life always
have more fun than the supercilious spectators."
~ William Feather

4

It's Okay To Feel Grumpy
Sometimes

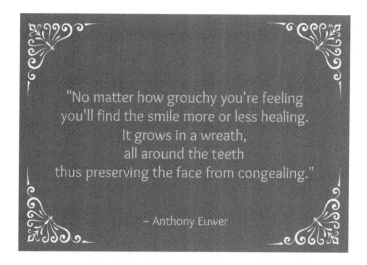

"No matter how grouchy you're feeling
you'll find the smile more or less healing.
It grows in a wreath,
all around the teeth
thus preserving the face from congealing."

– Anthony Euwer

In this chapter we'll look at why it's okay not to be a happy ray of sunshine all the time; that it's okay to occasionally feel grumpy and out of sorts. We'll identify powerful strategies and techniques for coping with times when you want to growl at yourself and those around you. You'll learn to identify and isolate the source of these feelings and move past those grumpy moments. Plus, we'll explore fun ways to give yourself personal time-outs, leaving you feeling refreshed and rejuvenated.

Coping Strategies for the 'Grrr' Times

All of us feel grumpy and out-of-sorts occasionally, and it's perfectly acceptable not to be a little ray of sunshine all the time.

A study conducted in Australia by Professor Joe Forgas determined that occasionally, feeling grumpy can actually be good for you. This study found that cheerfulness increased a person's creativity, while being grumpy increased careful thinking and attention to detail. The difference is actually determined by how the brain processes different information strategies.

Sometimes, when we're feeling bad all we want to do is shout, stamp, rant, sulk, mope and pout. It's good to get the negative feelings out in the open – give yourself permission to feel bad from time to time. Take a moment to stamp round the garden, pummel a cushion, shout at the TV, lock yourself in the bathroom, go to bed early, or whatever helps to express your frustration and let it out.

Be kind to those around you though, and explain that you need some space to deal with your emotions. Hopefully, after a while, you'll bore yourself with the grumps (before you bore everyone else around you as well!) and be ready to move on.

Obviously, constant negative emotions such as grumpiness will not help you feel good about yourself. Moreover, it will not make other people feel good about you either. Occasionally feeling down-in-the-dumps is perfectly acceptable and experienced by everyone. However, a constant or continual "growling at everyone" (including yourself) attitude should be examined for its source.

On any particular grumpy day, examine what's happened to make you feel that way. Determine if it's something you can or cannot control.

If a rainy day has dampened your mood, you might consider grabbing your rubber boots and going out to stomp in puddles, the way you did when you were a child. On snowy days, go outside and build a snowman.

"Attitudes are contagious.
Are yours worth catching?"
~ Dennis & Wendy Mannering

If someone said or did something that ruined your happy mood, evaluate their actions and reasons. It may be their world that's under a cloud and you just happened to get in the way. Try to shrug them off and move on to a sunnier spot.

When others make you grumpy:

- Were they intentionally being mean or was it unintentional grumpiness?
- How did you react, and why?
- Did you over-react or under-react?

- Was this an isolated event, or ongoing?
- What can you do to avoid any future recurrences?
- How can you move past this event?

*"The trick is to be grateful when your mood is high
and graceful when it is low."*
~ Richard Carlson

Mix It Up And Move On

One of the best remedies for grumpiness is to get stuck into some activities you enjoy.

When you feel fed-up and stagnant, you may be stuck in a pattern of negative behavior, made to feel grumpy by someone else, or trapped by a moment of grumpy self-indulgence. Challenge your thought processes and do something constructive to break out of it. If you're feeling overwhelmed, then do some small things that make you smile, tackle the grumps face on and do something different to get you buzzing again.

Mini mix ups

- Go for a brisk walk (borrow someone's dog if you don't have your own?).
- Take an invigorating shower/ wash away the grumps.

♥ Treat yourself to dinner at your favorite restaurant

♥ Call up a good friend and go to a movie (comedies are highly recommended!).

♥ Give yourself a gift – flowers, new lipstick, favorite
magazine, new book...

♥ Play loud music and dance until you fall over.

♥ Read a good book and break out the chocolate.

♥ Watch a feel-good movie, get an early night and wake up refreshed.

♥ Cook some comfort food, call a friend, and chat.

♥ Go shopping and buy those shoes you've been dreaming about for weeks.

Mega mix ups

♥ Book a holiday or take an unscheduled short break.

♥ Sign up for a new sport, or something that gives you an adrenaline rush.

♥ Apply for a new job/quit your job.

♥ Volunteer for something close to your heart.

♥ Redecorate your home.

♥ Join a drama group.

♥ Train for a marathon.

♥ Adopt a rescue dog.

♥ Sign up to a vocational program and expand your horizons.

These are example ideas for breaking out of a bad mood. As the saying goes – 'a change is as good as a rest'.

What ideas can you come up with that would lighten a grumpy mood and get you back to feeling good again?

"And that is how change happens.
One gesture. One person.
One moment at a time."
~ Libba Bray

Time-Out And Refreshers

Personal 'me-time' should be only about you and what you like to do (but sharing this with others can also be great). It can last an entire weekend, or only 10 minutes. Consider this as a time to refuel your energy; if your energy is low and your attitude is grumpy, take the time to refuel, reenergize and refocus.

Personal time-out is crucial, not only for grumpy days but also as regularly scheduled events.

Create a list of 10 activities to include as part of your personal time-out toolkit. Some relaxing ideas to consider may be:

- A picnic on the beach or in a nearby park.
- Meditation or yoga.
- Listening to uplifting music.
- A favorite hobby or crafting.
- A day at a spa.
- Going to that museum you always meant to visit.
- Soak in a candle lit bath with some relaxing music.
- Spending an hour (or more) reading with no interruptions (no phones, television, Internet).
- Applying a face mask or hot-oil hair conditioning treatment.
- Sitting on the porch and staring at the stars.

It's so important to take time to care for yourself, especially if you spend much of your time caring for others. You need to make sure you get enough rest, eat properly, and stop before you've had enough.

As the airlines say – first put on your own oxygen mask before you try to help others!

*"Loafing needs no explanation
and is its own excuse."
~ Christopher Morley*

5

Turn Your Dreams Into
A Reality

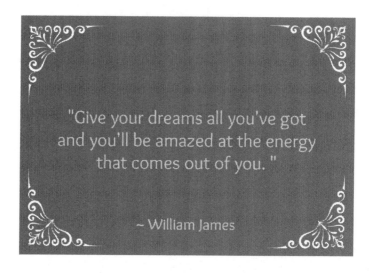

"Give your dreams all you've got
and you'll be amazed at the energy
that comes out of you. "

~ William James

*Everyone has dreams they would like to see become reality,
and in this chapter, you'll learn how to identify and assess
both your short and long-term goals and desires. You'll
discover how to focus on meaningful goal setting, how to
create a systematic plan to reach your goals, and how to
then turn those goals a reality.*

Everyone receives a fabulous boost when they've
successfully reached a goal or accomplished a meaningful

task they set for themselves. Identifying and turning your dreams into a reality is one of the best ways to feel amazingly good about yourself.

> *"The achievement of your goal is assured the*
> *moment you commit yourself to it."*
> *~ Mack R. Douglas*

Assessing Your Short And Long-Term Objectives

You may have short-term goals, such as learning to cook a new recipe, or a long-term goal such as graduating from a top cooking school. To get closer to achieving your goals, it's helpful to understand what motivates you to achieve them, the steps that need to be taken, and the time you'll need to allocate to these steps.

You may already have a very clear image of what your dreams look like, and how exactly you're going to turn them into reality. However, in case you need some inspiration, we'll explore some options to help get you on the right track toward actually fulfilling your dreams.

Short term goals focus on what you can achieve *right now.*

Make a list of the things that will motivate and inspire you, and that you know you'll feel great about achieving. Examples could include:

- ♥ Learning to crochet baby clothes for a new arrival.
- ♥ Saving up for a special outfit.
- ♥ Creating a website for your business.
- ♥ Completing a self-defense class.
- ♥ Starting a new language course.
- ♥ Creating an outline for a new book.
- ♥ Spending quality time with loved ones at the weekend.

Short-term goals can also be building blocks toward a long-term dream. For example learning a new language may be needed for a move to a new country. Creating your first website or learning a new skill maybe a single step in building toward a new career or business.

Long-term goals are about where you want to be/what you want the future to look like.

Your dreams will reflect your personal values and beliefs. They should be *your* dreams, not someone else's, although sharing a dream with someone can be hugely motivating. If your actions and your values are in conflict, your dreams will be impossible to achieve. Make sure your dreams truly reflect your values and your passions.

"We must never be afraid to go too far,
for success lies just beyond."
~ Marcel Proust

Are you clear on your long-term goals? If you need inspiration, consider some of the following to get your thoughts rolling:

- ♥ What personal talents do you have that you'd like to use?
- ♥ What hobbies are you passionate about and would love to work on?
- ♥ Is there a specific job you'd like to be doing or training you could sign up for?
- ♥ Are there people you'd like to spend more time with in the future?
- ♥ Are there places you'd like to visit or have more freedom to travel?
- ♥ Are there any big events you want to plan for such as a wedding?
- ♥ When you picture yourself in the future, what makes you smile and inspires you to work toward?

Now take your long-term goals and break them down into manageable bite-sized mini goals. Think about the individual steps you need to make, and write them down. Each one of these can then be tackled separately, with each mini achievement building toward to the end goal.

Finding A Way/Goal Setting

For goals to be achievable, they need to be measurable. Can you measure _your_ accomplishments in a specific manner, such as hours, weight, dollars, or miles? Having a measurable dream means you can actually track your progress until you reach your end goal.

By telling your brain precisely what you want to achieve, it will subconsciously help you to achieve your goals. Avoid general or vague terms such as 'more' or 'some' and instead, use specific terms. If you want to save money next month, specify the exact amount and what the money is for. If you want to lose weight, specify the exact number of pounds and when you want to lose them by.

Your brain is an amazing tool and has the capability to help you achieve almost any precisely outlined and realistic goal.

By using SMART objectives, you create an effective plan to help turn your dreams into reality:

Specific - clearly outline what needs to be achieved (learn French – speaking and writing)

Measurable – identify a measurable outcome (achieve a pass mark of 90%)

Achievable – can you commit to the task (6 months of evening classes?)

Realistic – do you have the recourses and support you need (course fees and baby-sitters)
Time specific – when the goal needs to be achieved by (complete by 31st December)

To turn your dreams into reality, it's really valuable to set out a clear plan and direction. Most importantly, your dreams must make sense to you; and remember - **they may be out of reach at the moment, but don't put them out of sight!**
A fundamental step to reaching your dreams and goals is to get them written down. These could take the form of motivational snapshots, which you see each morning when you wake up. Or they could be detailed outlines of the 'what, why, how and when' for each or your dreams. When you write your goals down and keep reviewing them, your brain recognizes their importance, and will focus on finding ways to help you achieve them.

"If you can dream it, you can do it."
~ Walt Disney

Making It Happen

So we've looked at identifying what your dreams look like and how to create a plan to achieve them. Now you need to focus on actually making them happen.
One powerful tip is to share your dreams with others; share them with people who you know will help motivate

and encourage you, especially if things get tough. When you share your dreams with family and friends, they will add their support and enthusiasm to yours. NOTE: Don't bother to share your dreams with negative people who are likely to discourage you.

It can also be really beneficial to find ways to make your goals tangible (i.e. something you can touch, see, smell or hear). Your brain cannot visualize "great cooking" but it can visualize a diploma from an elite cooking school.

Use your one or more of your senses to help motivate you:

- ♥ Create a 'dream-board' of images you'll see daily.
- ♥ Listen to CDs that reflect your desires and stir up positive emotions.
- ♥ Cook some special foods that remind you of a holiday you're planning.
- ♥ Use a lovely scented shower gel to help start your day with a zing.
- ♥ Place a bright colored doormat at your front door – this could trigger positive thoughts or reminders as you enter or leave your home.

What creative ways can you think of to stimulate your senses and keep you motivated toward your goals?

Your goals should always be positive. It's much easier to work toward positive outcomes, as opposed to away from a negative. Rather than say, 'I want to quit my boring job' focus on saying, 'I want to lean a new skill so I can do a job I really enjoy'. That way, you're not dwelling on the problem, but finding solutions to move you toward your dreams.

It's worth recognizing that your goals and dreams may change over time, which is perfectly natural. Be flexible and adapt your plans as necessary. You don't need to compromise on the outcome if that remains constant, but how you get there may need to be tweaked. Or you may find your circumstances change and you find yourself with a whole new set of dreams and desires.

Whatever form they take, your dreams are very significant to you. Your dreams should reflect something you truly want and desire. They must be something that will improve your life, and are worth fighting for.

Achieving these dreams may take hard work, concentration, and dedication, but, in turn, you'll feel so proud to have turned them into a reality.

"Success comes in cans not can'ts"
~ Author Unknown

6

Health and Wellbeing -
Getting The Right Balance

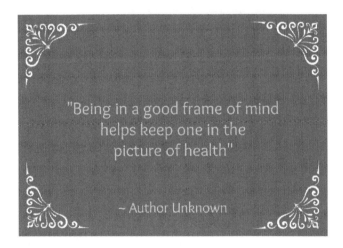

"Being in a good frame of mind
helps keep one in the
picture of health"

~ Author Unknown

Feeling good about yourself comes from both inside and out. In this chapter, we'll explore the significance of getting a good balance between the inner and outer self. You'll learn the importance of exercise, sleep patterns, diet and managing stress.

Additionally, this chapter will help you examine underlying physical and emotional issues that may be holding you back.

Feel Good Diet

Feeling good about yourself involves taking care of the inside. For example, if you eat foods which only provide "empty calories" (i.e. contain a lot of sugar or salt), you will find yourself feeling sluggish with no energy and no focus. That's not to say you should exclude all of your favorite treats, but enjoy them in moderation. Maybe only add that chocolate brownie covered in fudge sauce and topped with whipped cream to your time-out list instead of as a normal evening snack.

As with most things, a good, healthy diet offers variety, moderation, and balance. The proper balance of carbohydrates, fats, proteins, minerals and vitamins will help you look better and feel better about yourself. Deficiencies in certain essential vitamins, minerals and nutrients can lead to symptoms associated with physical diseases, stress and depression.

There is no 'one size fits all' diet that works miracles without some effort. Common sense should prevail and a nutritious, balanced diet (with a few treats thrown in) will make you feel (and look) a whole lot better than a poor quality diet full of sugary drinks and low nutrient foods.

"When it comes to eating right and exercising,
there is no 'I'll start tomorrow.' Tomorrow is disease"
~ Terri Guillemets

Good Mood Foods

What we eat can have a direct effect on how we feel. Certain foods can have a direct effect on our brain's ability to process signals for sleep, hunger, stress and moods.

The good news is that there are lots of foods that can help improve our moods and give a feel good boost. Foods that help you produce serotonin (a feel good hormone that can regulate moods and increase positivity) are a great place to start.

Foods that are great for a mood boost:

1/ B vitamins such as B6, B12 and folic acid can help fight depression and stress

Suggested Foods Packed With B Vitamins:

Brown rice, porridge oats, wholegrain bread, oatmeal, bananas, orange juice, baked potatoes with the skins, peppers, broccoli, asparagus, spinach, avocados, chickpeas, green beans, natural yoghurt, eggs, chicken, salmon, tuna, sardines

2/ Minerals such as magnesium, zinc, calcium and selenium are needed to counter stress and build a healthy immune system

Suggested Foods Packed With Minerals:

Brown rice, porridge oats, nuts – almonds/walnuts/brazil, seeds – pumpkin/ sunflower, garlic, peppers, broccoli, spinach, sunflower seeds, tofu, wild rice, tuna, salmon

3/ Specific proteins and carbohydrates promote the production of feel-good hormones such as serotonin
Suggested Foods Packed With Tryptophan:
These foods contain high levels of tryptophan which helps to create serotonin - walnuts, bananas, cottage cheese, cheese, eggs, beans, turkey, chicken, and fish

4/ Vitamin C can help boost your immune system
Suggested Foods Packed With Vitamin C:
Orange juice, strawberries, broccoli, brussels sprouts, peppers

...and to round things off, it's also great to know that small portions of dark chocolate can be a healthy good mood booster! Good quality dark chocolate is packed with antioxidants and phytonutrients, which are associated with a healthy heart and properties that fight cancer. Chocolate is known to stimulate the release of endorphins, which are feel-good hormones that help to promote a sense of well-being. **Who said diet had to be boring!**

Another important point in terms of diet and feeling good is to ensure you eat regularly. If you start the day well, with a nutritious, sustaining breakfast, then you'll have bags more energy, and be less likely to snack on rubbish foods.

Skipping meals can also be responsible for making you feel drained and tired because of a drop in blood sugar levels. Why play catch up and try to reverse a low mood or lack of energy, when some simple planning can keep you feeling good all day?

It's also worth noting the importance of water in terms of helping you to feel good. Regularly drinking water will not only keep you hydrated throughout the day but it has a load of other benefits as well. Water helps transport oxygen and energy to your cells, helps control your blood pressure, and electrolyte levels, flushes out toxins, and helps regulate your body temperature.

**Let's face it - the better your diet,
the better you'll feel each and every day!**

This book has only provided a basic overview of how diet can help you to feel good. There are loads of great books and advice available, if you want to carry out more detailed research on how specific foods can help you manage your moods and feel better. Just a few simple steps may be all that's needed to improve your diet and ensure the foods you eat help you to feel good about yourself.

According to Terri Guillemets, "You are as important to your health as it is to you".

Feel Good Exercise

As with the diet tips above, exercise can help increase your serotonin levels and can, therefore, improve your mood.

Getting enough exercise is one of those feel good essentials. Even something as simple as a brisk walk every day can do wonders for creating a positive outlook. It's also important to remember your body doesn't need to meet unrealistic standards set in magazines or television. Your body is unique and individual, and you should feel good about yourself just as you are, as long as you're looking after yourself as well as you can.

Ideally, regular, structured exercise programs are best, as they can help build stronger muscles, stronger bones and joints, provide protection from diseases, help control your weight, and slow down the aging process. Human bodies are structured to be very active, and when you participate in regular exercises that challenge your muscles, your body releases both growth and repair hormones.

Another great benefit from exercise is that it also releases natural chemicals that help to reduce stress and anxiety. Regular activity is a healing and preventative boost for not only your physical body, but also for emotional and mental health, enabling you to naturally feel good about yourself.

Achieving exercise goals or overcoming a physical challenge is a great way to boost your confidence. Plus, there's the added benefit that you'll be in better shape, which will show in your appearance.

Interestingly, studies have been conducted which show exercising outdoors has a much greater effect on improving mood than indoor exercises. Training whist being in a natural environment can bring a higher sense of satisfaction, plus increased enjoyment levels and happiness. If you feel more energized, then you're bound to feel more refreshed and, therefore, more motivated to keep doing more of the same.

Yoga is also a great way to help reduce stress, get in shape, and calm your mind. There are a multitude of health benefits, with studies showing that yoga is a safe way to increase physical activity, strengthen muscles, and increase flexibility and balance. Yoga is about practicing an overall healthy lifestyle, with improved body health, improved posture, and a chance to de-stress by un-cluttering your mind and getting your focus back.

Exercise is an individual choice, and can take the form of sports that get your heart pumping such as jogging, cycling, team sports, and going to the gym or similar. However you can also get involved with less intensive exercise such as going for brisk walk, mowing the lawn, washing the car, and doing the chores to lively music.

Anything that gets you moving regularly and increases your heart rate is likely to be good (subject to professional medical advice, especially if you have any health concerns).

Whatever your preferred style of exercise, it's worth considering a routine that will get you together with other like minded people. Their energy and encouragement can sometimes be just what you need to help motivate you and give you that desired mood boost.

Tips to getting more exercise:

- ♥ Add your exercise goals to your short-term goals list.
- ♥ Set an alarm clock daily (for any time of day) to remind you to get started.
- ♥ Book a class and pay for it. You've paid, so you may as well go!
- ♥ Tell people about your new commitment. You're less likely to quit.
- ♥ Link it to an event such as a charity run.
- ♥ Find a fitness buddy so you can motivate each other.
- ♥ Link it to a specific reason (e.g. 'get into a size smaller jeans for holiday').
- ♥ Hang the size smaller jeans outside your wardrobe as a visual motivator.

- ❤ Pin a physical picture of your ideal outcome to the bathroom mirror.
- ❤ Take measurements and track your progress - seeing improvements is highly motivational.

"In order to change we must be sick and tired
of being sick and tired."
~ Author Unknown

Sleep To Feel Good

In addition to exercise, sleep is a vital element to getting a balance of inner and outer health.

Lack of sleep can result in "grumpy" days, with moodiness, impatience, irritability, and an inability to concentrate for any length of time. A lack of sleep reduces the brains ability to remember and learn new skills. People who regularly suffer from a lack of sleep have an increased risk of anxiety and depression, and an increased risk of developing immune deficiency and heart disease. When you're tired, your brain will focus on your body's immediate needs, and will not be focused on helping to achieve your dreams and goals.

Poor sleep can have a major impact on our daily lives, affecting our relationships, our health, our ability to concentrate, and our moods.

Knowing how vital it is to get enough regular sleep is one thing. But what do we need to do to achieve it?

Try some relaxing bedtime tips to wind down and prepare for sleep:

♥ Have a warm bath with a relaxing essential oil such as lavender.

♥ Drink a small amount of warm milk.

♥ Listen to some relaxing, slow music.

♥ Write down your 'To-Do' list for the next day so things won't play on your mind.

♥ Read a chapter of a book via some low level lighting.

♥ Deep, slow breathing, focusing on relaxing your muscles.

Things to avoid

♥ Rigorous exercise before bedtime (e.g. running or the gym).

♥ Caffeine drinks before bed.

♥ Hot, stuffy bedroom – sleep is enhanced with a cool, well ventilated room.

♥ Heavy, rich or spicy foods at least two hours before bed.

♥ Drinking too much liquid close to bedtime.

♥ Using technology directly before bedtime, as it can over stimulate your brain.

♥ A bad bed – make sure your mattress and pillow are supportive and comfortable.

Extra Sleep tips:

- Be consistent. Not always possible, but your body responds better to routine.
- Go to bed the same time each night, and get up the same time each morning.
- Try an earlier bedtime if you're struggling to get up in the morning.
- A daytime nap can help, but evening ones may prevent you sleeping later on.
- Sleep swaps - arrange regular nights where the kids stay over at friends/relatives. Return the favor and you'll all benefit from some extra shut eye.
- Check your pillow is supportive and comfortable, and covers not too heavy or light.
- Keep your room dark during the night and cover up any intrusive light displays.
- Try focusing on muscle relaxation for each part of your body as you drift off.

With busy, hectic lives, sleep is not always easy to come by. However, by understanding the damage you can cause from long-term sleep issues, then finding solutions to achieve an adequate amount seem obvious. Many of these self-help tips can work well, especially if combined, and you make them a genuine health goal.

However, if you've tried various techniques and you are still struggling, then don't discount seeking professional advice. You may need some extra help with getting on top of sleep issues, so you can support yourself and feel as good as possible.

Stress Tips

"To avoid sickness eat less;
to prolong life worry less."
~ Chu Hui Weng

We all need some stress in our lives; the trick is to not let it get out of control.

Good stress can help stimulate us, make us more effective, and perform at a higher level. A burst of hormones in the right situation can help us focus and get things done quickly. Plus it can be a healthy state for your body to be in, providing it's not prolonged.

However, if your body is awash with stress hormones for long periods, then it becomes a problem. Long-term stress can lead to high blood pressure, fatigue, insomnia and depression amongst other health issues. You may find that you suffer with more illnesses such as colds and flu as a result of your immune system being suppressed.

You may feel overwhelmed, anxious, moody, miserable, frustrated, agitated, and struggle to relax or unwind. Being over-stressed can often make you feel bad about yourself, resulting in low self-esteem and depression.

Assessing the causes of your stress can be a valuable step toward managing the symptoms.

Think about *your* 'Stress Causes'

- Who or what specifically causes your stress?
- How do you react to these stressful events/people?
- How do you feel physically and emotionally when this stress occurs?
- How long do those symptoms last?
- When do these symptoms subside (and do you know what alleviates them?)?

One technique you can use to reduce stressful situations is by utilizing The Four A's – **avoid, alter, adapt and accept.**

- You can help **avoid** stress by learning to say "no" and by avoiding the people and situations that cause your stress. Reduce your daily "to-do" list and designate items as "must do" or "should do" or "can be eliminated."

♥ You can **alter** situations that cause stress by managing your time more effectively, by expressing your feelings rather than keeping them bottled up inside, and by being more assertive and dealing with problems head-on.

♥ You can **adapt** to whatever or whoever is causing your stress by assessing at the big picture, and looking at things from a different perspective. Will this stressful situation matter in a week/month/year, and is it really worth being upset over?

♥ You can learn to **accept** what you can't control or change, instead focusing on what you can alter. Make an effort to look at every stressful situation as an opportunity to grow, or to learn something new. Learn to share your feelings and learn to accept. Focus on releasing negative energy and just move on.

Where possible, we should try to change the way our brains react to stress, for example by practicing meditation, deep breathing and getting regular exercise. Even moderate exercise can help to reduce the stress hormones, making your mind and body more resistant to harmful emotional stresses.

Try some stress-reducing tips to help you relax:

- Calm down – close your eyes, relax your body, and take slow, deep breaths.
- Focus on the positive – identify and be grateful for the all good things in your life.
- Concentrate on positive thoughts and words. When you're feeling negative you may say harsh words to both yourself and others. Replace with positive ones.
- Exercise – go for a brisk walk to blow away the cobwebs, or sign up to a yoga class to take control of on going stresses.
- Look to the future – see yourself in a better place and keep that picture in your mind's eye.
- Do something – don't sit around and feel bad, engage in some uplifting activities.
- Take time out – be caring toward yourself, take time to relax and do things you enjoy.
- Connect with others – seek out the company of positive people. Having supportive friends can mean the world.
- Be more tolerant – remember that others may be stressed too, don't judge too harshly.
- Get more sleep – it's hard to cope with stress when you're also exhausted from a lack of sleep.

- ♥ Talk it through – by expressing your worries and talking them through with someone else, they can seem more manageable.
- ♥ See the bigger picture – in a month's time, will this really matter? If you don't achieve X, will the world stop turning?

Which ever way we choose to manage or reduce stress, the objective shouldn't be its complete absence. Stress is an unavoidable part of reality. The trick is to avoid becoming overwhelmed by the events or people in our lives, to take control of our feelings and responses, and to proactively manage these occurrences.

Hopefully, you'll find ways to control your stress levels. However, sometimes there are underlying issues that would be better served by the attention of a health care professional. It's not always possible to find our own solutions to problems, and we may need more than deep breathing exercises. Do whatever you need to get you back on the right path, and to a place where you can feel good about yourself.

"The best six doctors anywhere
And no one can deny it
Are sunshine, water, rest, and air
Exercise and diet.
These six will gladly you attend
If only you are willing
Your mind they'll ease
Your will they'll mend
And charge you not a shilling."

Nursery rhyme quoted by Wayne Fields

7

It's Okay To Ask For Help

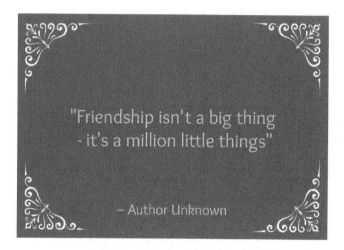

"Friendship isn't a big thing
- it's a million little things"

– Author Unknown

For many of us, asking for help can be hard to do. In this chapter we'll discuss the reasons why we can find it so difficult, and how to identify the circumstances where you're best off seeking support. We'll look at how and when to ask for assistance, and explore areas where help is available.

By examining your specific needs, you'll be able to determine when the best time to ask for help is, and who are the right people to ask.

When And How To Ask

For many of us, it's often difficult to reach out and ask for help. It may feel like an admission of failure or that you're weak in some way. The truth is all of us need help from time to time - don't be too proud to ask, or be concerned that it shows weakness. Don't wait until a situation becomes completely overwhelming; ask for help as soon as you realize you need assistance.

Don't get sidetracked by feeling guilty or embarrassed. Realizing you need help, and then asking for it, is often the wisest and most successful strategy, saving time and reducing stress. You'll find a great sense of relief once you acknowledge you need help, and proactively find a solution.

The most valuable step in asking for help is to define exactly what you need, and then thinking through any ideas to solve that requirement. With your needs defined, you'll gain a better insight into who or what might be able to help. Consider everyone you know, or could make contact with, to determine who might have relevant experience, knowledge or time to support you.

What help could you benefit from, if you had a magic helper?

- Someone to mow the lawn/walk the dog/pick up some shopping

- ♥ Baby sitting while you attend a class
- ♥ Learn to use the Internet
- ♥ Medical information or treatment
- ♥ Collect the kids after school
- ♥ DIY jobs round the home
- ♥ Financial support
- ♥ Someone to talk to
- ♥ Get sufficient sleep
- ♥ Advice or information
- ♥ Write a resume
- ♥ Quit smoking
- ♥ Parental advice
- ♥ Spiritual or personal guidance
- ♥ Someone to drive you when there's no public transport
- ♥ A fitness buddy

If you feel uncomfortable asking someone initially, you might find it easier to write down your request first to clarify your thoughts. Explain the problem to yourself, how you think it could be resolved, why it's important to you, and how a particular person or solution can help. Once you are comfortable with this, you could also practice how it sounds with a friend or family member, if it seems appropriate. Ask them for any positive feedback to help improve your request.

When asking for help, always be very polite and do your best not to seem whiny or too desperate. Thank the source of help in advance for any assistance they can provide, and be understanding if they can't help. Most times, people are more than willing to lend a helping hand. Sometimes, you only need to ask.

"It is not so much our friends' help that helps us
As the confident knowledge that they will help us."
~ Epicurus

There are occasions when you hope that someone will help you, and yet, they seem unreasonable in their refusal or they let you down. Unfortunately, this happens to all of us and it's just part of life. If that happens to you, then try to get past the frustration and rule them out from asking again in the future. There are other people out there who are reliable and happy to help, so focus on them instead.

Recognizing that you have the skills to know when and how to ask for help, and the courage to actually ask, can greatly reduce stress in your life. Make sure you're also available to provide help to others as and when required and this can make you feel really good about yourself.

As James Durst says, "Help one another; there's no time like the present and no present like the time".

Different Types Of Support

Religious And spiritual Leaders Or Groups

Depending on what's important to you, and your personal beliefs, you may find it beneficial to seek support from a religious or spiritual leader or group. There are multiple benefits to be gained from seeking support in these areas, especially in terms of connecting with like-minded people and learning more about yourself.

Religious and spiritual leaders are often able to provide you with access to specific services, direction, guidance, and advice when you need it. These types of services may not be easily found elsewhere, so consider what options are available to you in your local area.

Co-workers

There are often times at work when we need help. It could be that we're inundated with tasks, or we lack the skill to complete something or to move forward. Asking for support from a colleague or your boss can have benefits for both you and your employer, as you'll become more productive as a result of the help.

Just make sure you ask at an appropriate time, be clear on what you need and why, and what the benefits will be to everyone involved. Hopefully, you'll be pleasantly surprised at the outcome.

Friends And Family

Good friends and supportive family are worth their weight in gold. When you find yourself in need of emotional or physical help, it's great to know they're there for you. Make sure that you recognize and thank them for their support and return the favor as often as possible.

However, it can be hard to deal with family or friends who are less than supportive, and make your life more difficult than it need be.

If you can't get help from these people, look elsewhere. Don't waste spend time fretting about what they don't offer, instead find others who will bring value to your life and let them know how important to you they are. Seek out new friendships where possible, and create fresh opportunities to meet people – healthy, supportive friendships can blossom in all sorts of places.

Local, County, State Or Federal Government

Depending on where you live and your personal circumstances, you may find help available from government sources. Support can be provided in the form of financial assistance, or a range of local community services.

The Internet or your local library is a good starting point to find out more about the services or public programs you could access.

Librarians can also offer a wealth of information about resources that may be available to you, especially in the local area.

Health Care Providers

There are many areas where you can find support for health related issues, both public and private, depending on your needs and circumstances. Health workers such as dentists, physicians, dietitians, pharmacists, therapists, nurses and social workers can offer numerous solutions and benefits.

You could also consider solutions offered by alternative medicines and treatments such as chiropractic, acupuncture, reiki or homeopathy.

Health concerns, whether physical or emotional, should be addressed as soon as possible to help you feel at your best.

Seeking support and taking control of your health issues is an important part of self-caring and getting to feel good about yourself.

Local Community Organizations

There's likely to be a wealth of opportunity to become involved with local community groups or activities. Some of these maybe government run, some nonprofit organizations, some independent or some may require a paid membership.

Whatever your interests or needs are, there's bound to be some local groups you can become involved with. Many are actively looking for new members, and you may be able to offer them support and skills that they can benefit from too.

Volunteering in your local community is another way to broaden your support network. As well as introducing you to new people with shared interests, community groups often offer access to neighborhood resources which you otherwise may not know about.

Internet Community

Additionally, the Internet offers an alternative way to access support groups or source information. There are many active communities of people with common interests or goals, and you can interact with people from all over the world at the click of button.

If it's information you're after, then the Internet is often the best place to start searching for answers. Try a Google search and see what you can come up with!

Yourself

Learning to support yourself may sound clichéd, but it works. By removing, or moving around obstacles and becoming solution oriented, you *will* move forward. All of the above can offer potential support, friendship and solutions. However, you need to actively seek out the answers.

Resolve to find ways to move closer to your desired outcome, and you should be rewarded with some great results.

Be your own best helper, and make things happen.

"Friends are those rare people who ask how we are, and then wait to hear the answer."
~ Ed Cunningham

8

Clear It Out

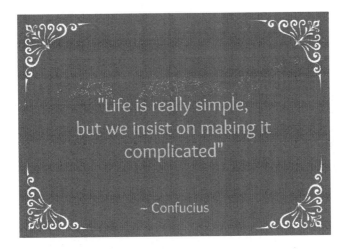

"Life is really simple, but we insist on making it complicated"

~ Confucius

Our lives are filled with unnecessary "stuff", which can cause stress, anger and frustration. In this chapter you'll learn to de-clutter and clear it all out. We'll look at the skills necessary to carefully examine all the clutter in your life – in your home, car, desk, wallet, purse, and in your mind. You'll discover the fine art of de-cluttering and how to get rid of all of the superfluous stuff.

Plus, we'll also explore the effect of negative, "toxic" people you encounter, and learn how to clear them out of your life.

De-clutter Yourself And Your Surroundings

We all find ourselves swamped with clutter at times; mental, emotional or physical clutter. Clutter can be both a cause and a symptom of stress in your life, and will distract you from accomplishing what you really need to be doing. Living with clutter can be frustrating, making you feel overwhelmed and buried beneath a mess.

The act of clearing out any type of clutter starts with small steps and a positive mindset. You need to **sort, simplify, organize, and clear it out.**

For a physical de-cluttering project tackle each area separately such as your bathroom, kitchen, bedroom, office, garage, car, shed, and so on.

- ♥ Begin by clearing away everything on the floor.
- ♥ Next, work on flat surfaces such as counters and shelves.
- ♥ Then, move to the furniture, drawers and closets.
- ♥ Have a selection of storage boxes/ files at hand as you sort through.
- ♥ Sort everything into separate piles - throw out, keep, or donate.
- ♥ Make your throw out pile an actual trash bag, so you are not tempted to go through the pile and reclaim items.

It may help to have a friend, family member, or co-worker help you with a de-cluttering project. It'll make you think twice when they ask you, "Why in the world are you keeping that!?"

Any clutter you decide to keep should be organized and stored neatly in cabinets, closets, or drawers, where it is handy, but not visible. Tackle your de-cluttering projects one room at a time. When all of the physical de-cluttering has been accomplished, step back, congratulate yourself, and enjoy the new space.

One sure fire way to feel good about your efforts is to donate any spare items to charity. There's plenty of donation bins or stores to choose from, so do them a favor and pass on your unwanted items.

You'll soon feel fabulous for getting rid of all this stuff, and creating a clear, clean and organized space.

Unfortunately though, de-cluttering isn't a one-off event. The process of de-cluttering and becoming organized takes up front effort and an ongoing commitment. However, creating a clear space can mean a simpler, easier way to live. Developing systems to stay organized and clutter free means you'll have more time to do things you enjoy and concentrate on making yourself feel good.

Extra tips for successful de-cluttering:

- ♥ Find a place and system to deal with incoming paperwork – deal with items daily and they won't build up.
- ♥ Choose 3 items each day from a messy area and find a place for them.
- ♥ Keep picking one small area - a drawer, shelf, or bathroom cupboard. Rotate and stay on top of the clearing and cleaning.
- ♥ Plan a de-cluttering weekend – set aside specific time to tackle the bigger projects.
- ♥ Don't over-complicate it – take 15 minutes each day and dedicate them to a de-cluttering project. You'll be surprised by the cumulative results!
- ♥ Work through your wardrobe – e.g. week 1 - go through your shirts, week 2 - pants, week 3 - underwear and so on, until you've eliminated down to the items you actually wear.
- ♥ Keep a charity bag at the ready. When you find stuff that needs to go, pop it straight in the bag and forget about it until you're ready to drop by a charity store.
- ♥ Set up some simple systems - create a dedicated place for bills, bank statements, correspondence, etc and file your paperwork straight away.
- ♥ File quickly. Once you've created your simple filing systems, you just need to use them.

♥ Get everyone on board. Ask everyone to make an effort - if you clear up daily, then it won't build up to a mammoth task again.

The next step is to de-clutter your life and lifestyle. Explore all the different aspects of your life (home, school, work, family, hobbies, etc.) and consider all of your commitments. Write down these commitments, separated into the categories listed above. **WARNING! Actually seeing all of your commitments written down might be a bit scary!**

Review your lists and identify any commitments that can be reduced or eliminated. This is also a great incentive for learning to say "no".

With your lists completed, review your schedule and your daily routine. You can be more productive, and reduce stress, when you actively organize and schedule your activities. Group together similar tasks, by location or type. For example, schedule grocery shopping once a week, rather than every night after work. Try and arrange tasks such a collecting the dry cleaning, popping to the chemist, and dropping something round to a friend all in the same run, if possible.

Plan out both daily and weekly schedules. Write them down and stick them in a place you'll see each day (and where you'll pay attention to, not just glimpse at). Follow your schedule as closely as possible, being mindful that it will need to be revised and changed several times before you reach maximum efficiency and minimum clutter.

Seeing how much you can accomplish by following an organized schedule can help you feel more in control. Plus, you'll be able to identify some time slots you can use for some lovely, feel-good, personal time-outs.

"A place for everything and everything in its place."
~ Charles A. Goodrich

Toxic People

There's one more really important area, which you may need to examine closely and then clean out. Just as you avoid having toxic substances in your home or workplace, you need to avoid toxic people in your life.

Toxic people are those who add no real value to your well-being, or who actively seek to cause you harm. They may be 'friends', co-workers, neighbors, associates, or relatives. These are people who are constantly complaining, demanding, or just being plain nasty. Toxic people may be selfish, jealous, uncaring, unfeeling, silent, unsupportive, rude, and maybe even aggressive.

Identify if you have any toxic people in your life, and to what extent they affect you? When a person has always been unpleasant, or for any extended length of time, the cause is likely to be down to their own personal issues, and not because of anything significant you've done (even though they may perceive things otherwise).

These people need to be kept out of your life as much as possible.

> *"Toxic people will pollute everything around them.*
> *Don't hesitate. Fumigate."*
> *~ Mandy Hale*

If a normally pleasant person has recently become unpleasant, consider what may have happened in their lives to bring about this change. For these people, you may want to exercise some patience and understanding, in the hope that their pleasant personality reemerges.

There are two basic methods for
removing toxic people from your life;
one is easy, but less direct, and
one is more difficult, but more honest.

Firstly, you can simply stop any contact with the toxic person; stop taking and returning phone calls and/or emails. You can stop visiting, stop going to places where that person is likely to be, and make excuses if that person happens to confront you about your sudden unavailability. Although you may not feel as good about yourself if you go this route, it can be highly effective, and may be the best solution for certain circumstances.

Secondly, the more difficult removal method is to directly confront the toxic person. Try and explain why you are having an issue with their behavior and ask/or state what needs to done to change the situation. It's possible that they are unaware of the horrible effect they're having, or they have their own resentments that need to be aired. However, if there is no amicable way to resolve their unpleasant attitude, then let them know that that you'll no longer be spending time with them, and tell them why.

Be prepared to offer a few examples of their toxic behavior and the affect it has on you and/or others, especially if they ask – and they probably will. Be calm, polite, concise and clear, remaining firm in your actions. You should be ready for them to react in a variety of ways, such as crying, denial, yelling, or anger - and be ready to receive a laundry list of your own shortcomings. React politely and end the conversation as quickly as possible.

Ideally, this is not something you should do over the phone or in writing. As hard as it will be, in person is the best method. A public place might be a good location for such an encounter, especially if there is any possibility of aggressive behavior.

You may never hear from this person again. Or, they might contact you immediately, acting as if the entire confrontation never happened, or they may try to engage in further confrontation. Unless their attitude has changed, you need to remind them of your feelings, and discontinue contact.

It's possible that the toxic person may express sincere regret over their previous behavior. You'll need to decide if you believe their apology is truly heart-felt and you are both able to move on, or if there is too much history and risk of receiving more toxicity if you remain in contact.

A particularly difficult situation occurs when the toxic people in your life are your relatives. The complete cut-off method will seldom work, but the face-to-face confrontation may be a solution or, at the very least, reducing contact as much as possible. Try to have some ready made reasons as to why you need to cut the visit/call short, and have this in your armory for each time their behavior begins to become toxic. If you're lucky, they may just take the hint, but if not, you have a ready made excuse to get out as quickly as possible.

Be aware that any removal of contact involving family members can cause additional problems elsewhere in your life. Tread softly here, and go as far as you can to protect yourself, whilst not causing too much of a detriment elsewhere in the family.

"Life is amazingly good when it's simple
and amazingly simple when it's good."
~ Terri Guillemets

9

Smiling, Laughing and
The Fun Stuff

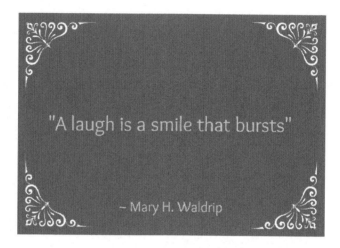

"A laugh is a smile that bursts"

~ Mary H. Waldrip

In this chapter, we'll examine the immense benefits that come from smiling, laughing and generally having fun. You'll see how volunteering and giving of your time is a great way to make yourself smile. Then, we'll look at writing a prescription for a daily dose of smiling, laughter and fun.

Smiles And Laughter

You've probably heard both of these sayings "A smile is contagious!" and "Laughter is the best medicine." Both of these are absolutely true. Simply by smiling, you instantly feel better in yourself. Scientific research has shown that simply using the facial muscles to smile can help improve your mood. This is because your brain interprets the fact that you're smiling as meaning you're happy and feeling good. Even faked smiles can help kick start a good mood.

Smiling makes our brain think we are happy. When our brain thinks we are happy, we tend to smile more. This result is referred to as the "facial feedback loop" and it can help to make you feel good about yourself and the world around you.

> *"Every time you smile at someone,*
> *it is an act of love,*
> *a gift to that person,*
> *a beautiful thing."*
> *~ Mother Teresa*

Laughter will often follow smiling. People around you will want to share in the happy experience. Meaning everyone gets to participate in the feel good factor. Such a simple action can improve the mood of everyone in your vicinity – so smile and share in the laughter.

Enhancing your sense of humor, and learning to laugh more – especially to laugh at yourself – will improve both your mental and physical health, and your overall outlook. Unlike the drawbacks of spending time with toxic people, spending time with people who make you smile and laugh is amazingly beneficial.

Laughter will not only improve your mood, but it also reduces tension and stress in your body. When you laugh, your brain releases endorphins, chemicals that help you relax and trigger a sense of well-being. Laughter also helps to improve your immune system, and humor in general can help trigger your creative side.

Along with releasing feel-good endorphins, laughter expands your lungs, replenishes the oxygen in your lungs, and releases pent-up emotions. Laughter is not only good medicine, it's also wonderful exercise. According to Maciej Buchowski, a university researcher, laughing for 10-15 minutes can burn around 50 calories.

"Laughter is a tranquillizer
with no side effects."
~ Arnold Glasgow

Volunteering And Giving

Volunteering
When you volunteer your time and efforts for a worthwhile cause, you've found an awesome way to make yourself and others smile.

Volunteering is a great way to make new friends and meet interesting people, as you're sharing activities with others who have a common interest. Volunteering can also help you to become involved with the local or wider community, and can help develop your own support network.

There's a whole range of activities you can become involved with such as one to one support, driving, or fundraising, through to physical activities such as gardening, caring or dog walking. Whatever type of role interests you, there's bound to be something you can become involved with, which will inevitably provide you with fun and fulfilling activities.

Another great benefit to volunteering is that it can give you a fabulous boost to your self-confidence and overall sense of satisfaction in life. When you're part of something good, and you know you're helping others, you can be proud of your own achievements.

And after all, the stronger the image you have about yourself, the easier it is to feel positive about yourself in the long term.

Giving Of Yourself

There are many ways you can gift a part of yourself, and in so doing, add incredible value to the lives of those you care about.

For example, you can give your time, trust, commitment, loyalty, energy, enthusiasm, respect, and so on. Or, you may choose to give money to a worthwhile cause, a struggling family member, or as a gift.

Often, we don't realize the importance of giving away these intangibles, yet they can be extremely powerful gifts to give.

How many ways can you think of to give a gift of yourself?

- ♥ Give your kids your complete attention as they tell you about their day.
- ♥ Place trust in someone who's earned it.
- ♥ Be respectful toward others by showing them kindness.
- ♥ Give passion and energy to the relationship with your partner.
- ♥ Listen closely, without interruption, when someone tells you something important.
- ♥ Commit to spending quality, fun time with your partner.
- ♥ Give a compliment to a stranger.
- ♥ Smile and let your loved ones see how much you cherish them.
- ♥ Drop in on an elderly neighbor and check they're okay.
- ♥ Be enthusiastic and encouraging to friend who shares a personal goal with you.
- ♥ Donate your time to a worthwhile cause.

- ♥ Set aside time to do some fun stuff with just you and the kids.
- ♥ Give your all to an important project.

There are so many ways we can demonstrate our support, friendship, love, and caring toward others. These gifts will benefit the recipients in many ways, and hopefully, they will be keen to share in a similar way.

It's also important to remember to share these gifts with yourself as well, showing yourself a high level of respect and value.

When you make others feel special, and you treat yourself with a good dose of self-respect, you can't help but feel great about yourself.

> *"Kindness in words creates confidence.*
> *Kindness in thinking creates profoundness.*
> *Kindness in giving creates love."*
> *~ Lao Tzu*

Fun Stuff

Having fun is a big part of being able to smile and laugh as often as possible. People are attracted to others who are smiling because they appear more approachable and nonthreatening, making people who laugh and have a cheerful demeanor a desired part of any group or event.

Ideas to increase the fun quota in your life:

- ♥ Re-live some fun activities you enjoyed as a child. Go to a park and jump on the swings, or try the circus or amusement park.

- ♥ Stick funny cartoons, jokes and sayings around your home or office. Add these funny items to a file so you can review them whenever you need a pick-me-up.

- ♥ Take a stressful situation and turn it into a sitcom.
  Exaggerate the situation, making it bigger and bigger. Make yourself the hero of the hour and single-handedly resolve this larger-than-life problem. You'll be surprised how absurd the situation appears, and how good you feel about yourself for handling it like a super hero!

- ♥ Set up a treasure hunt – works for any age group!

- ♥ Attend local comedy or theatrical shows (maybe participate, if given the opportunity).

- ♥ Visit a 'pick-your-own' fruit farm and stock up.

- ♥ Whatever your age, invite your friends for a slumber party. Eat junk food, stay up late watching rom-coms or telling creepy stories. Encourage everyone to bring along a stuffed toy to snuggle.

- ♥ Bake some cookies and take round to friends or neighbors to share or swap.

- ♥ Play board games or cards and make the losers take on the household chores.
- ♥ Organize a pamper party and have some girlie fun (guys included too, if they want to show their softer side).
- ♥ Cook marshmallows on an open fire.
- ♥ Organize a fancy dress party.
- ♥ Dig out some old music or movies and have a retro evening.

"Growing old is mandatory. Growing up is optional."
~ Chili Davis

Write yourself a prescription for a daily dose of smiles, laughter and fun. Post the prescription where you see it first thing each morning (perhaps with a photo of you pulling a silly face!) and make it an essential part of your day.

Build a "Things That Make Me Smile and Laugh" list:

- ♥ Spending time with cheery friends and relatives.
- ♥ Sharing jokes or funny stories.
- ♥ Watching the sunset/sunrise.
- ♥ Going out to get ice cream.
- ♥ Reading a funny book or comic.
- ♥ Creating a Pinterest Board of funny pictures or sayings.
- ♥ Watching YouTube videos of funny animals
- ♥ Giving a belly rub to your pet.
- ♥ Getting out and being silly (throw a Frisbee round the park).
- ♥ Get baking with friends or the kids and make a mess.
- ♥ Singing loudly or dancing wildly

Make a commitment to laugh, smile and be silly - you'll be amazed at how good you can feel!

"A good laugh and a long sleep are the best cures in the doctor's book."
~ Irish Proverb

10

The Fabulous You

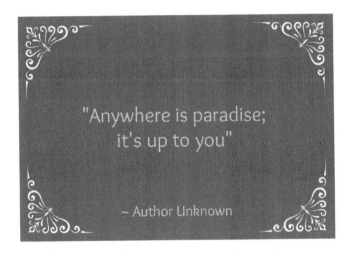

"Anywhere is paradise; it's up to you"

– Author Unknown

We all have a fabulous us inside, and in this chapter you'll discover how to bring out that amazing person. We'll explore techniques to build self-confidence, plus look at how other people see you, and how that compares to the way you see yourself.

We'll also examine how and why you should make a big investment in yourself, so you can be as truly fabulous as you possibly can.

Confidence Techniques

We all have an amazing, fabulous person inside. The trick is to believe in ourselves enough to let the world see that person as we'd like them to.

The issue that holds most people back is a lack of confidence or low self-esteem. Get this licked and you're on the way to feeling good about yourself whenever and wherever.

> ### _So what do you need to do to look, feel and act confident?_

There are many confidence-building techniques you can work on, and we've identified some that can make a huge difference:

- ♥ **Take control.** Ultimately _you_ are the only one in control of you, and you need to commit to working on the areas that will improve your self-belief.
- ♥ **Practice saying "no"** to the stuff that adds no value to your life. Practice saying "yes" to the things that will benefit you. Fight the fear and do it anyway.
- ♥ **Stop procrastinating** (think being in control). Finish all those projects you started, or ditch them. Decide on what's worth your time and

effort and get them done, or eliminate them completely so they don't clutter up your mind.

♥ **Wear it well.** What you wear and how you wear it says a lot. Mix it up with bright colors. Understand what styles and outfits work well on you and wear them with pride. Ask others for advice or treat yourself to a day with a stylist. And don't underestimate the power of a good hair style. We all feel better when we have a great hair day!

♥ **Think positively** and act positively, ditch the negative. Ban self-defeating words or negative thoughts toward others. Be solution oriented. Use your energy to be proactive and focus on the good as much as possible.

♥ **Speak with confidence.** Be clear and positive. Don't mumble, repeat yourself, or keep apologizing. Be genuinely interested in others.

♥ **Stop picking on yourself.** You're a good person and you deserve respect. Treat yourself right, block/reverse any negative thoughts toward yourself, and be kind.

♥ **Head up, shoulders back.** Walk tall. Smile and make eye contact. A straight posture and assured walk do wonders for your appearance, and how others perceive you. Plus, good posture helps lift your mood and energy levels.

- ♥ **Increase your knowledge**. Broaden your horizons. Learn new skills. As you grow, you'll develop confidence in new areas.
- ♥ **Set mini goals** and make them happen. Quickly move past any failures. Focus on easy wins. Keep celebrating these successes. The bigger wins will follow.
- ♥ **Get out**. Exercise. Meet people. Try something new. Get out of your comfort zone – you'll be amazed at what you can do and how good that makes you feel.
- ♥ **Play to your strengths**. If you're good at it or love it, do more. Use your natural strengths and talents to benefit yourself and others. Share - don't keep them hidden.
- ♥ **Be authentic**. Stick to your principles. Act with integrity. You know what's right for you, so be proud of who you are and believe in your decisions.

You can look and feel more confident just by embracing some of these techniques.

When you behave in a confident manner, others will soon perceive you in that way. In turn, you'll feel more confident, expand your level of self-belief, and receive a tremendous boost to your self esteem. It's also important to always recognize your successes, celebrate your talents, make the most of everything around you, and to value yourself as a fabulous individual. ***After all, you're amazing!***

> *"Be proud to wear you."*
> *~ Dodinsky*

How Do You And Others See Yourself?

How self-aware are you and what level of self-esteem do you have? If you struggle with a poor self-image, then you will struggle to ever feel good about yourself.

> *"So many of us invest a fortune making ourselves*
> *look good to the world, yet inside we are falling apart.*
> *It's time to invest on the inside."*
> *~ Iyanla Vanzant*

Our self-esteem is based on how we think others see us. Their opinions can deeply affect the way we view and value ourselves. A negative self-perception is both harmful and unwarranted.

So how much time and energy
do you spend being concerned
about what other people think of you?

Allowing others to define us, in a negative context, can block us from feeling confident and good about ourselves.

Developing a high level of self-awareness allows you to understand yourself better, and, therefore, interpret how others see you. By better understanding our own personalities, behaviors, emotional reactions, beliefs, motivations, thought patterns, strengths/ weaknesses, and likes/dislikes, we are able to control how others see us. Equally, we can control how much value we place on their opinion of us.

Enhancing your self-awareness can be a healthy step toward boosting your confidence, and allowing others to perceive you as you would like them to. When you're comfortable with who you are and how you respond in certain situations, then your self-esteem is in a good place, and you'll feel good about yourself.

Building self-awareness is an ongoing journey, and starts by focusing on the various elements of your personality, your behaviors and emotional responses. You need to be conscious of your thoughts and reactions, and how they affect you and others around you.

Observe and question yourself:

- Were you happy with your behavior in a given situation, or could you have managed things differently?
- Was your response appropriate, or could it have been better?

- What beliefs do you have that shape the world around you?
- What emotions do you experience in certain situations, and are you able to control your emotional responses?
- What are you passionate about or what motivates you to do better/more?
- Are you clear on what you like/dislike, and communicating that to others?
- Can you make a long list of your strengths and how to put them to good use?
- Can you list areas of your behavior or skills you'd like to improve upon?
- Is your personality geared toward risk taking, or are you more comfortable with lower risk activities?

Observe and understand yourself. Accept that you are allowed to feel and react in your own way. Make a decision and action plan to work on areas of your behavior or responses you're not happy with.

Try and see yourself as an outside observer:

- Do you mumble quietly or speak clearly and articulately?

- Do you speak loud and fast, or in a controlled manner?
- Do you wear clothes that make you look good or hide away in shapeless stuff?
- Do you stoop or walk tall?
- Do you state your opinion firmly while respecting the views of others?
- Do you get stuck into activities or hang back and wait?
- Are you supportive of others or self-absorbed?
- Are you easy to be around, or needy and difficult?
- Are you quick to judge or tolerant of others?
- Do you smile and make eye contact, or avoid interacting?

Try and view yourself as a friend or stranger would - observe the way you interact with others. Are people comfortable around you, or are there aspects of your behavior you could improve upon? Are you hard to communicate with, too needy or clingy, high maintenance, moody, demanding of attention, disrespectful of others opinions, reserved and unapproachable, or openly demonstrating your insecurities?

None of us are perfect, and we should not need to apologize for who we are. However, there are times when our behaviors cause problems for both others and ourselves, and to move forward, we need to modify the way we act. Recognizing the issues is the first step to taking control. By developing methods to adjust our unsatisfactory behaviors, we can make ourselves far more pleasant to be around. Others will respond to us in a positive way, which, in turn, will help to build our confidence and then make us feel good about ourselves.

Life is not a race and you can improve things as you go along. In the meantime, by understanding and accepting who you are, you will project a more confident image to the world. How we think others see us is important to most of us. However, we can control parts of this by adjusting our behavior and responses. For the remaining part, we have to accept and like ourselves for who we are.

**One thing's for sure –
you can't please everyone in life.**

However, if you see yourself in a positive light, are doing your best, and are happy with yourself, then the rest doesn't matter.

Be yourself, be amazing.

*"When there is no enemy within,
the enemies outside cannot hurt you."
~ African Proverb*

Self-Investment And Personal Development

One of the best investments you'll ever make is in yourself. By improving your knowledge and skills, you'll enhance your life and benefit the lives of those you care about as well.

When you think about your aims and motivations in life, what do you see as your ideal future? By developing your know-how and skill set, you're investing in your future potential. When you empower yourself with worthwhile goals and achievements, you are able to make better choices in the future.

Personal development can take many forms, depending on your aspirations and interests. The 'investment' does not necessarily require a lot of financial costs, as there are many free or low cost methods available.

Here are a few development ideas to consider:

- ♥ Develop employment skills and confidence in the workplace - volunteer to take on extra tasks or responsibilities outside of your general remit
- ♥ Work toward a promotion, career progression or self-employed potential
- ♥ Learn new social and communication skills
- ♥ Improve existing talents and strengths or work on areas of weakness

- ♥ Learn to play an instrument.
- ♥ Work toward a healthier lifestyle.
- ♥ Take up a new sport.
- ♥ Learn to run your own successful business or enterprise.
- ♥ Develop self awareness and self esteem building techniques.
- ♥ Learn how to invest wisely for your financial future.
- ♥ Work toward a professional qualification.
- ♥ Attend an assertion class.
- ♥ Religious or spiritual growth.
- ♥ Improve your confidence and project a stronger image to the world.
- ♥ Develop a hobby or lifestyle choice.

Personal development and the time you take to invest in yourself should be a lifelong journey. Why stagnate when there's so much to enjoy and get involved with? Even if you have an extremely busy lifestyle, it's important to take time to focus on goals that can *improve the lives of both you and your loved ones.*

> *"Lend yourself to others,*
> *but give yourself to yourself."*
> ~ *Michel de Montaigne*

As your self-confidence and happiness grows, the self-confidence and happiness of the people around you grows, and that adds to your own self-confidence and happiness, and so on. We come back to another feedback loop.

And remember; you are unique.
No one else can ever be
exactly like you, or you like them.

<u>**Make the most of yourself**</u>
<u>**and make it count!**</u>

By identifying and releasing the fabulous you inside, you can accomplish whatever your dreams may be. When you know you're fabulous both inside and out, you definitely have to feel great about yourself.

"If we all did the things we are capable of doing,
we would literally astound ourselves."
~ Thomas Alva Edison

11

Helpful Habits For Achieving Daily Positivity

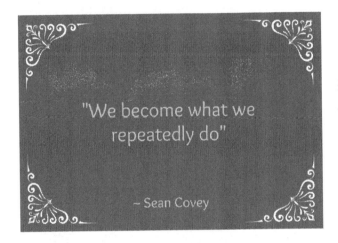

"We become what we repeatedly do"

~ Sean Covey

In this chapter, we'll explore the valuable habits you can build to achieve daily positivity, allowing you to feel great. You'll learn how and why to make time for yourself – without feeling the least bit guilty! You'll discover the benefits of saying "thanks" and being grateful for what you have and what you receive.

Plus, we'll look at creating bite-sized pieces of happiness to keep you motivated and feeling good about yourself.

Our daily lives are influenced by the habits we've developed. Over time we develop both good and bad habits. There are neutral habits such as taking out the garbage on a set day, bad habits such as chewing our nails, and good habits like cleaning our teeth twice a day.

One of the essentials to feeling good about yourself is to reduce your bad habits and increase the time you spend on the beneficial ones. Building positive new habits is not always easy (although can be surprisingly simple in many cases) but worth the effort. Each time you develop a valuable habit, you're adding to the ways in which you'll feel positive about yourself.

Constructive new habits don't need to be complicated. They could be as simple as remembering to smile at yourself in the mirror, taking a piece of fruit to work instead of cookies, complimenting a loved one or reading a chapter from a motivational book each day.

Try not to take on too many at the same time or you'll confuse yourself, and write them down as a prompt until they become a natural part of your daily routine. Stick notes on the mirror, fridge, bed side table, or wherever you'll see them as a daily reminder.

"Let go of your old tired habits
and plant new habits in fertile soil."
~ Harley King

Getting Up Earlier

This may sound easy and yet, in reality, can seem hard to achieve. Many of us are already getting up 'early', so waking even earlier can seem daunting.

However, rising early can be an effective way to start your day, for many reasons:

- ♥ You have the chance to set the tone for a positive day.
- ♥ There are fewer distractions around at that time.
- ♥ Take mini moments of 'me-time' and enjoy the peace and quiet.
- ♥ There's opportunity to clarify and focus your priorities and goals for the day.
- ♥ Once fully awake, your brain should be more productive and creative.
- ♥ Previous night preparation = jump straight in to whatever you've planned.
- ♥ You can enjoy the sunrise!

Take your time to build up to earlier starts, so you don't become discouraged or fall back into your old routine. Your body clock may need time to adjust to get the most benefit from a new early-bird start to the day.

Like any worthwhile habit, you should find that the benefits are numerous. If you have a good enough reason to motivate you, then you'll find a way. The extra productivity alone should be enough to boost your mood for the rest of the day. If in doubt, try it – you might really enjoy it!

> *"Early to bed and early to rise makes a man*
> *healthy, wealthy and wise."*
> *~ Ben Franklin*

Being Thankful, Grateful And Appreciative

By appreciating what we do have, and not focusing on what we don't yet have, then we are already in a more positive mindset.

Studies have shown that people who regularly express gratitude are happier, more optimistic, and have a greater outlook on life. People who practice being thankful are less likely to suffer from stress or depression and have a better sense of control in their life.

There are many ways to express your gratitude, from daily thoughts, to prayer or meditation.

How do you express gratitude in your life?

By focusing on the good things, both large and small, we can alleviate negativity and boost our mood immediately. When we pay attention to the positive things in life, our brains become attuned to focusing on the things we find to be valuable. We then start to see more and more reasons to express our gratitude.

"Do not take anything for granted –
not one smile or one person
Or one rainbow or one breath,
or one night in your cozy bed."
~ Terri Guillemets

Tips on how to voice gratitude:

- ♥ Keep a 'gratitude journal'. Note down *all* the things in your life, both large and very small, that you are thankful for.
- ♥ Add to your journal daily with at least 3 new things you've appreciated.
- ♥ As you go to sleep, examine your gratitude list – your subconscious will thank you for the lovely positive thoughts.
- ♥ Put time aside for mediation or prayer.
- ♥ Take a moment when waiting for the kettle to boil to smile and think through the day's best bits.

There can be so many things to be grateful for, both small and large. In a busy world, things can often seem insignificant. Yet, when we actively name them and recognize their value, we bring them into clear focus.

Examples of what we could be thankful for:

- ♥ Our health and wellbeing, and that of our loved ones.
- ♥ Our home and our safe return.
- ♥ The people in our lives we care about
- ♥ The times we are able to spend with friends and loved ones.
- ♥ Someone who reached out to us in a dark place.
- ♥ The company and love our pets give us.
- ♥ Someone's kind words or compliment.
- ♥ A neighbor who unexpectedly helped us out.
- ♥ The 'me-time' you found and used to relax and pamper yourself.
- ♥ A good night's sleep.
- ♥ Helpful advice you received just when you needed it.
- ♥ A smile from someone when you were having a bad day.
- ♥ Money we can put away in to savings
- ♥ A lost item that found its way back to you.
- ♥ Enjoying a nice meal.
- ♥ A sunny day or rain when it's needed.

We should also remember to say thanks to ourselves. If you've made a brave decision, been kind to someone, been assertive, complimented a friend, taken control, helped someone out, achieved a goal, and so on, then add yourself to the gratitude list.

Saying thanks to the world, and acknowledging your own accomplishments, is a great way to feel good and stay positive.

"God gave you a gift of 86,400 seconds today.
Have you used one to say 'thank you'?"
~ William A. Ward

Relaxing And Time Out

An important part of the feel good factor is learning how to relax, and take time out.

There are various relaxation techniques around, and you may need to try a few to identify which ones work the best for you. Your level of fitness, lifestyle requirements, and personal preferences are relevant to finding which ones are motivating and effective.

If you're feeling stressed, tense, or anxious, spending time engaged in relaxation techniques can work wonders to restore your inner peace and balance. And the good news is, most of these are easily accessible and cheap to do.

Many of these can be carried out at home in your own time, or you may prefer the benefits offered by attending a class, especially if you're just starting out.

Examples of relaxation techniques:

- ♥ Relaxed breathing technique.
- ♥ Deep muscle relaxation.
- ♥ Therapeutic massage, reflexology or reiki.
- ♥ Meditation or prayer.
- ♥ Yoga or tai chi.
- ♥ Creative activities such as painting, woodwork, knitting and playing music.
- ♥ Gentle exercise such as walking, swimming, cycling, gardening or jogging.

The style of relaxation technique may differ; however, the benefits are largely the same. The key benefits are that they can lower stress, improve concentration, and help to improve a number of mental and physical health issues. Speak to your health care provider first, if you have any significant health concerns though, before you jump into any new activity.

Psychological benefits can range from a boost in self-confidence, peace of mind, clarity and focus, positivity, and an increase in self-awareness and perspective on life's stresses. The more you practice, the greater the overall benefits.

"You should sit in meditation for twenty minutes
every day – unless you're too busy;
then you should sit for an hour."
~ Old Zen adage

In addition to these techniques, there are many other ways to grab some time to relax and zone out. Mini bites of 'me-time' can be precious and an essential part of feeling good.

Take time out to chill and unwind:

- Run a warm bath, add essential oils, spa-like music and apply a face mask.
- Dim the lights and play some soft music.
- Head out for a walk through the woods or by the river.
- Sit quietly and practice deep breathing.
- Find somewhere quiet to get lost in a good book.
- Wander around the garden.
- Give yourself a mini mani/pedi treatment.
- Do something repetitive but enjoyable to switch off your busy brain.
- Stretch your muscles, loosen any tension, and massage the knotty bits.

♥ Snuggle up with a hot water bottle, a warm drink and watch a favorite movie.

Hopefully, you will have restored a sense of calm and balance. Taking time out to specifically relax and rejuvenate is an important step to feeling good about yourself. Your emotional well-being shouldn't be taken lightly, and anything you can do regularly to improve your emotional and physical health should be high on the agenda.

Techniques such as yoga and meditation can teach you to relax and retain the calm feeling throughout the day. Give them a go – add them to your goodie bag of 'feel-good tricks'.

"Sometimes the most important thing in a
whole day is the rest we take
between two deep breaths."
~ Etty Hilleum

Bite Sized Pieces Of Happiness

Helpful habits come in many forms and we've taken a look at some of the positive ones you can begin to cultivate. However, feeling good about yourself and learning to *stay* positive is not always easy, and sometimes, we find ourselves down in the dumps. When this happens, it's helpful to have a list of 'go to' activities you can throw yourself into.

Whether you need to blast away some negativity or top up your feel good vibe, **here's some bite sized bits of happiness to consider:**

- ♥ Head out with your camera and take some happy snaps.
- ♥ Create a home spa – soak, buff, condition and wallow.
- ♥ Get creative – paint, cook, write, garden, knit, or whatever you fancy.
- ♥ Put on your glad rags and hit the town.
- ♥ Pack a picnic and eat yummy stuff alfresco.
- ♥ Buy flowers – they look great and energize your home.
- ♥ Try a new hair style or color.
- ♥ Lose yourself in a good book (or 2 or 3).
- ♥ Book tickets to a gig, the theater or a movie.
- ♥ Grow your own veggies – they taste great, they're free, and how clever will you feel!?
- ♥ Snuggle down with a DVD and popcorn for an afternoon of movies.
- ♥ Get active and feel the adrenaline rush.
- ♥ Head out to your favorite restaurant.
- ♥ Be spontaneous – don't plan it, just do it.
- ♥ Go have some playtime...

What else can you come with? Try to ensure you have some feel good essentials on your 'To-Do' list. That way, you'll be on the right track to achieve a daily dose of positivity without any effort!

"Be happy with who you are and what you do,
and you can do anything you want."
~ Steve Maraboli

12

Making The 'Feel Good Factor' Last

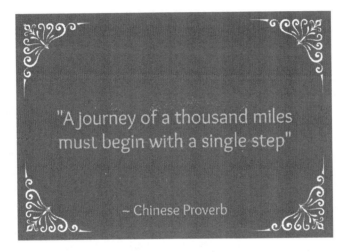

"A journey of a thousand miles must begin with a single step"

– Chinese Proverb

So what do the happy, confident, outgoing people have in common? They have a well-balanced sense of self-belief and self-worth. Underneath, they are no better or more capable than you or me. However, genuinely happy people have managed to accept themselves for who they are, and learned a set of values that allow them to feel relaxed, secure, and content with themselves.

Many times, people who exude lots of confidence are covering up their personal insecurities. Most people experience self-doubt or confidence issues at various time in their lives – it's perfectly natural. It's just that some people learned to mask them well or actively manage them, when others can be overwhelmed by them.

Not everyone has the good fortune to be surrounded by a great set of circumstances, or loving, supportive friends and family. However, those who allow negative circumstances and/or other people to define their world for any significant length of time, will struggle to break away from the negativity trap.

Recognizing the source of personal issues, understanding the necessary steps to gain control, and then taking meaningful action is the key to moving past these issues. It can take great strength and courage to move from a place of hardship or crushing low self-esteem. However, when you resolve to tackle your problems, and actively seek solutions, you'll empower yourself to create positive changes in your life.

"The flower that blooms in adversity is the rarest and most beautiful of all"
~ Author Unknown

So....

Throughout this book, we've looked at techniques you can use to help feel good about yourself, boost your mood, and get to a place of permanent daily positivity.

We've explored how to:

- ♥ Get out of your own way and unlock the fabulous you.
- ♥ Focus on events and situations you can control, and let go of those you can't.
- ♥ Say *NO* to requests as and when *you* want to.
- ♥ Have more fun by saying *YES.*
- ♥ Be grumpy and out-of sorts from time to time.
- ♥ Find personal 'me-time' and why it's so valuable.
- ♥ Identify your goals/dreams and turn them into a reality.
- ♥ Set both short and long-term goals.
- ♥ Create a balanced approach to nutrition, health and well-being.
- ♥ Incorporate exercise, sleep, and stress management into your life and why they're essential.
- ♥ Ask for help and feel good about it.
- ♥ Evaluate the physical and mental clutter in your life and clear it out.
- ♥ Identify and neutralize toxic people.
- ♥ Write a prescription for a daily dosage of smiles, laughter and fun.

Self-help books will often offer information that can sound great but then just stop there. Throughout this book we've tried to highlight some of the incredible steps you can take toward feeling good, including practical steps to take away and practice.

The concepts may not be revolutionary, and you may have come across some of them before. However, the key to achieving the feel good factor and boosting your happy hormones is to highlight the ones that work for you, consistently take action, and make them part of your daily routine.

If you've ever tried to use methods to feel good, but then given up because you think they're not working, then you may need to try a different approach. You probably need to deal with the basics first, and identify the issues which are truly holding you back, and preventing you from feeling good about yourself.

When you delve into your deepest issues, and understand the reasons as to why you don't feel good about yourself, then you're in a much stronger position to find the best solutions to fix them. Dealing with these issues, and finding methods to move past them, will have the biggest impact on your self-esteem and confidence.

Define what 'feeling good' means to you

Does it look like family approval, acknowledgement of your feelings/views, external recognition, sporting or career success, or a quiet internal comfort? When you're comfortable and content with who you are, the voices of others who try and define, control or direct you are not important.

Identify where *your* pressure points are:

- Critical parents
- Competitive siblings
- Jealous colleagues
- Narcissistic friend
- Weight and self-image
- Demanding boss
- Belittling partner
- Bullies
- Judging yourself against others
- Stuck in the past
- Low self-worth
- Medical issues
- Rude hurtful people
- Unsupportive family
- Not fitting in
- Negative self-talk

You need to find a way to process, manage, and move past negative feelings such as hurt, disappointment, suffering, dissatisfaction, sadness, rejection, pain, anger, embarrassment, shame, or not being good enough. These feelings are a natural part of being human but over time, will erode your feelings of self-worth and the ability to be relaxed, confident, and to stay in a happy place.

> *"Don't water your weeds."*
> *~Harvey Mackay*

You may find that one day, you just wake up and are ready to say "Enough of the negativity!" You draw a mental line (or a physical one, if you like visual imagery), step over it, and get on with being a brand new you. No more tolerating other people's garbage, negativity, or meanness - "If you don't like me then that's your problem, *not* mine!"

Or you may start by practicing small steps, and building up to the harder steps as you begin to see positive results. You might find that external help would be a good decision for you, to best support you with moving forward. Which ever way you choose, you'll most likely need to actively work at managing these processes to see long term positive results.

Unfortunately, there's no one-size-fits-all solution, or quick fix options to help you feel good about yourself in the long run. It's about understanding your own pressure-points, working with the methods that are best suited to you, interpreting them in your own way and repeating them until you unconsciously begin to feel amazing.

When you alter your internal messages and shift your thinking to a place of self-value, then you can move from focusing on the positive steps to being on autopilot for feeling good.

Take Consistent Action

Pick out the steps you like best.
Print them out.
Practice them daily.

The fact that you were born into this world and are able to be here reading this book is an amazing fact in itself. Make the most of your opportunity on this planet to be the person you really are, and be proud of that unique and wonderful person.

Focus on ways to release any unhappiness, discontentment, disappointment and self-doubt. Practice, practice, practice until you reach a place where you are comfortable with yourself, content with who and how you are, and confident to keep building toward a better future.

Be proud of all your achievements along the way, both the mini steps and the large obstacles you climb over. Keep the momentum going and you'll make significant improvements in your ability to feel good about yourself in the long-term.

Take time to cherish all the good things in life, especially the people you care about and who care about you.

And remember, there are so many fabulous things you can do in life - places you can go, skills to learn, sports to try, people to meet, hobbies to start – the possibilities are endless.

> *"Life is too short to waste.*
> *Dreams are fulfilled only through action,*
> *not through endless planning to take action."*
> *~ David J. Schwartz*

You can delve into areas of self-discovery, learn how to take control of your life and find ways to boost your self-confidence beyond your wildest expectations. By making yourself a life-long leaner, you'll keep discovering new and exciting things about yourself and others. You have every right to feel fabulous and there's no time like the present to get started.

Feeling good about yourself is one of the best gifts you can give to yourself.

And there's only one person who can really make the difference - that's YOU. Good luck on your adventures - go ahead, make some amazing stuff happen, and see how fabulous you feel...

13

About The Author

Rachel Robins is the creator behind the feelfabtoday products. She has a passion for exploring and sharing ideas that centre on positivity & self improvement.

Rachel focuses her attention on how to help others feel as good as possible - using realistic feel-good techniques, healthy tips & a hefty dose of positivity. At the heart of the feelfabtoday products are methods on how to feel fabulous, look great, achieve more & live positively. These products are created with the help of a small team of talented people, who add their wisdom, knowledge and skills to the process, and who Rachel would like to thank for their continued efforts and support.

Rachel has worked in various senior management roles, where she's successfully practiced the art of conflict management, leadership, negotiation and change management, plus she's trained many teams and individuals to achieve successful, target driven outcomes. Her range of interpersonal skills, life experience and self-help knowledge means she's able to share practical steps on how to take control of your life, develop a positive self image, and feel good about yourself.

She's put together this FeelFabToday Guide on how to *Feel Good About Yourself*, so others can discover how to banish negativity, create instant mood boosts and achieve daily positivity.

Rachel's also written additional FeelFabToday Guides, designed to explore different areas of self empowerment, confidence building and feeling good about yourself. More information on these Guides can be found at **www.feelfabtoday.com**.

14

And Finally

We really hope you found this book to be helpful.

We'd love it if you'd also join us at:
https://twitter.com/feelfabtoday
http://www.feelfabtoday.com

**Many thanks for reading our book -
we wish you every success in achieving
your daily positivity...**

Thank You

Made in the USA
San Bernardino, CA
20 April 2017